FORAGING MUSHROOMS OF THE ROCKY MOUNTAINS

FORAGING MUSHROOMS OF THE ROCKY MOUNTAINS

Finding, Identifying, and Preparing
Edible Wild Mushrooms

**Colorado Mycological Society
Pikes Peak Mycological Society
Edited by Ed Lubow**

ESSEX, CONNECTICUT

FALCONGUIDES®

An imprint of Globe Pequot, the trade division of The Rowman & Littlefield Publishing Group, Inc.
4501 Forbes Blvd., Ste. 200
Lanham, MD 20706
www.rowman.com

Falcon and FalconGuides are registered trademarks and Make Adventure Your Story is a trademark
of The Rowman & Littlefield Publishing Group, Inc.

Distributed by NATIONAL BOOK NETWORK

Photos by Ed Lubow unless otherwise noted.
Additional photos provided by Alexis Murray, Alex Merryman, Ginger McKey, Ian Fierman, Jacob Ronder,
James Chelin, Jennifer Bell, Joseph O'Halloron, Maia Reed, Patricia Bukur, Ron Wolf, Roy Halling, Orion
Aon, Saadia Naiman, James Lentz, Jennifer Bell, Nicklaus Watson, and Ikuko Lubow.

Map by Melissa Baker and The Rowman & Littlefield Publishing Group, Inc.

British Library Cataloguing-in-Publication Information Available

Library of Congress Cataloging in Publication Data available

Names: Colorado Mycological Society, author. | Pikes Peak Mycological Society, author. | Lubow, Ed, editor.
Title: Foraging mushrooms of the Rocky Mountains : finding, identifying, and preparing edible wild
mushrooms / Colorado Mycological Society and Pikes Peak Mycological Society, edited by Ed Lubow.
Other titles: Falcon Guide.
Description: Essex, Connecticut : Falcon Guides, [2024] | Series: Falcon Guides | Includes bibliographical
references and index. | Summary: "Foraging Mushrooms of the Rocky Mountains provides detailed
descriptions of edible mushrooms; tips on finding, preparing, and using mushrooms; a glossary of botanical
terms; color photos"—Provided by publisher.
Identifiers: LCCN 2023042731 (print) | LCCN 2023042732 (ebook) | ISBN 9781493073825 (pbk) | ISBN
9781493073832 (epub)
Subjects: LCSH: Mushrooms—Rocky Mountains—Identification. | Cooking (Mushrooms)—Rocky
Mountains. | Edible mushrooms—Rocky Mountains.
Classification: LCC QK605.5.R6 .C65 2024 (print) | LCC QK605.5.R6 (ebook) | DDC 579.60978—
dc23/eng/20231129
LC record available at https://lccn.loc.gov/2023042731
LC ebook record available at https://lccn.loc.gov/2023042732

♾™ The paper used in this publication meets the minimum requirements of American National Standard
for Information Sciences—Permanence of Paper for Printed Library Materials, ANSI/NISO Z39.48-1992.

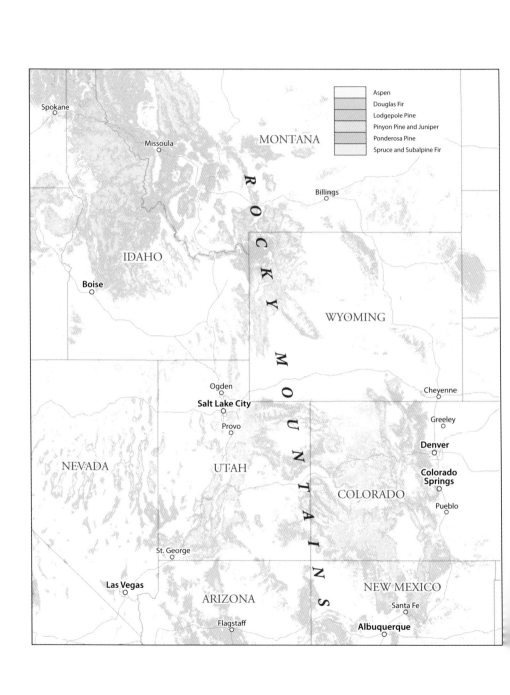

	Aspen
	Douglas Fir
	Lodgepole Pine
	Pinyon Pine and Juniper
	Ponderosa Pine
	Spruce and Subalpine Fir

Spokane

MONTANA

Missoula

R
O
C
K
Y

Billings

IDAHO

M
O
U
N
T
A
I
N
S

Boise

WYOMING

Cheyenne

Ogden

Salt Lake City

Greeley

Provo

Denver

NEVADA

UTAH

COLORADO

Colorado
Springs

Pueblo

St. George

Las Vegas

ARIZONA

NEW MEXICO

Santa Fe

Flagstaff

Albuquerque

CONTENTS

CONTRIBUTORS

These are the various people that contributed to the creation of this book:

Orion Aon
Jennifer Bell
Trent Blizzard
Miyako Boyett
Patricia Bukur
Dr. Alexander Cauley
James Chelin
Ian Fierman
Roy E. Halling
Michael B. Heim
Natalie Hyde
James Lentz
Ed Lubow
Ikuko Lubow
Ginger McKey
Alex Merryman
Alexis Murray
Saadia Naiman
Joseph O'Hallaron
Maia Reed
Jacob Ronder
Jon Sommer
Nicklaus Watson
Ron Wolf

COLORADO MYCOLOGICAL SOCIETY

In 1964 Dr. Sam Mitchel founded the Colorado Mycological Society (CMS), with Sam as the first president, Mary Wells as vice president, and Rosa-Lee Brace as secretary, treasurer, and editor of the newsletter. As of early 2023, the membership of CMS is over 1,200.

The original purpose of CMS was educational and to provide collections of fungi to the new fungal herbarium at Denver Botanic Gardens. The current mission statement of the society is: "We discover, photograph, identify, collect and preserve mushrooms. We savor those that are edible and cherish those that are not. We are dedicated to protecting mycological habitats as we enjoy nature's bounty. We wish to share our knowledge and experiences through education, expanding the understanding of our science. All the while, we strive to keep the fun in fungi."

In the 1970s, Manny and Joanne Salzman organized the first Mushroom Fair, held at Denver Botanic Gardens. In August CMS holds an annual Mushroom Fair at which hundreds of mushroom collections are brought in, identified, and displayed for the public to see. Many of these collections are added to the Sam Mitchel Herbarium of Fungi.

The club has four times hosted the annual Foray of the North American Mycological Association (www.namyco.org), in 1983, 1997, 2010, and 2021.

Monthly meetings are held from March through October, usually on the evening of the second Monday of each month. The subjects covered by the speakers are varied, recent topics including medicinal mushrooms, dyeing fabrics using mushrooms, mycoremediation, and ecological trends of fungi in the region.

PIKES PEAK MYCOLOGICAL SOCIETY

by Jennifer Bell

The Pikes Peak Mycological Society was founded by botanist Athalie Lee Barzee in 1974. She dragged her kids and anyone else who could keep up with her through the forests and fields of the southern front range of Colorado hunting for rare plants. Eventually she decided that mushrooms were more mysterious and rarer still!

Our focus today hasn't changed much. We are not an ivory tower club. Our goal is to meet the people of this area where they are: on the trails, in the kitchens, with the kids and dogs. We bring the mushrooms to young students at the yearly Cool Science Festival at UCCS. We show people how to prepare edible mushrooms at the annual Cook and Taste. We offer free, unusual classes of all kinds like how to teach your dog to help you find things in the woods and how to take photographs of fungi that glow in the dark. We look at mushroom DNA in mycology workshops and we lead forays every summer in the Pikes Peak region and at the Telluride Mushroom Festival.

Our high mountain region ranges in elevation from the 6,000 feet (riparian) all the way up to the tree line, which is just under 12,000 feet. We can experience it all in one day. Mushroom hunting season in the shadow of Pikes Peak is short, sweet, and intense.

Join your local mycological society.

It's the best money you will ever spend!

INTRODUCTION

Welcome to the world of foraging for mushrooms.

Foraging consists of hunting and gathering something, mushrooms in this case, for use as food or medicine. A mushroom hunt is commonly called a foray.

The purpose of this book is to provide an easy introduction for beginners into the world of mushroom hunting. Most people that hunt mushrooms are doing it to find something extra special to add to their meals. Most of the rest are seeking medicinal mushrooms. This book was written to help you do this safely and improve your chances for success.

One other difference between this book and others is that it was written by many authors from the Colorado Mycological Society and Pikes Peak Mycological Society, with the proceeds from the book going to support those groups rather than the individual authors. So you will see a variety of different writing styles which have been somewhat stuffed into a similar format for each mushroom.

It also serves as an introduction into some of what you can learn by joining one of the mycological societies above (or another if you live too far away). Groups such as these are the best way for most people to get into mushroom

Foragers about to set out. CREDIT: JAMES CHELIN

hunting. An Internet search will lead you to their web pages where you can find out more about them.

Tips for Using This Guide

You should actually read all of this introduction. If you haven't foraged for mushrooms before, this basic information will help you avoid rookie mistakes and get things right the first time. Even if you have hunted for mushrooms before, you may find some valuable tips to improve the way you forage.

This book will not teach you how to identify mushrooms accurately. Experience shows that the descriptions written in books, regardless of the level of detail, will be commonly interpreted by readers in overly optimistic ways. Photographs are a great help, but only if you know what details in the photo are important. This is not to say that the descriptions or photographs in this book are lacking; it's more to say that the intent of this book is not to teach mushroom identification.

If you want to learn to identify mushrooms accurately, take a class or go on forays with experienced people. Mycological societies such as the two mentioned earlier in this book will provide both of these. The best way to learn a mushroom species is to have a specimen in hand and an experienced person to point out the important things.

The many authors of this book are experienced mushroom hunters,

Striking gold in the forest. CREDIT: JAMES CHELIN

Go on forays with experienced people to learn to identify mushrooms properly. CREDIT: IKUKO LUBOW

and they are sharing their knowledge here. Some of it may seem obvious, but there are those for whom it is not.

Remember, you are the one responsible for what you put in your mouth. None of those responsible for writing this book can be liable because you decide to eat the wrong mushroom. Even edible mushrooms will make some people sick. Only you can prevent your own mushroom poisoning.

How to Foray

You have probably been out for a hike and seen lots of mushrooms and maybe collected some. If so, you've already been on a foray! There are a few extra things you should do for a foray that you probably wouldn't normally do just for a hike.

Decide where you want to go. Some places you can hike are not going to work for a foray. It is illegal to hunt mushrooms in any state or national park or monument. There are sometimes more local regulations that prohibit mushroom hunting. For example, it is illegal to hunt mushrooms in any Jefferson County open space. Some districts in the national forests require permits. As of the time of this writing the only ones requiring a permit are Dillon and Brecken-ridge. The permits are free and you need only visit the ranger station once a year to obtain your permit. If a permit is required, you will need a permit for each individual. Any limits on what may be collected will be written on the permit. On a recent permit the limits were 67 pounds per year and 5 gallons per day. You should also not trespass on private land. Ask permission before foraging on private property.

Found one! CREDIT: JACOB RONDER

A massive haul of king boletes. CREDIT: JACOB RONDER

If you're going to an area that a lot of people go to, you should consider leaving the mushrooms alone there so others may enjoy them, too. Finally, it's a good idea if somebody who's not going with you knows where you're going and when you expect to return. Also, leave a note on your car saying where you will be foraging and when you expect to return. Do not assume that you will be able to use your mobile phone in case of an emergency. Millions of acres in the Rockies are still beyond the reach of cell phone signals.

Make sure you can get there and back again. Sometimes roads or locations are closed for a variety of reasons, and driving for an hour or three only to find that your planned foray location is closed can make for a bad day. Allow for the possibility that the road may be in worse shape than last time. Often an Internet search will alert you about this.

Go with a group. If you're alone in the woods and something goes wrong the situation can be far worse than if you have at least one companion. It's also generally just more fun to share the experience with others.

Bring the equipment you need or want. There is a later section that goes into some detail on things you might want to bring.

Be alert for things you should avoid. Along the front range poison ivy is a common hazard. In many areas, so are rattlesnakes. Wild animals will normally avoid being near people, and being in a group and

Share the fun with the others in your group.
CREDIT: ALEX MERRYMAN

Do not approach wildlife, especially the big ones.

chatting as you hunt is a great way to make sure the animals hear you coming. Abandoned mines are dangerous, and their tailings can render normally edible mushrooms toxic.

When you find something, call the others in your group to come and see. Take some pictures. Before you take your find with you, check for insect larvae and make sure it's actually worth the effort.

Insect larva tunnels are usually pretty easy to spot.
CREDIT: IKUKO LUBOW

The larvae can tunnel from one mushroom into the others next to it and also ruin those. Don't waste time collecting small mushrooms for eating unless there are a lot of them. Almost all mushrooms shrink when cooked. How many of those mushrooms will it take for a single spoonful?

As a general rule, if you find a mushroom, it's your mushroom. Don't poach other people's mushrooms, and you should probably get permission from them to even pick up the mushroom, much less cut it open or do anything else.

As you collect, either be sure to try to identify what you're collecting, or keep the entire mushroom so it can be identified later. When foraging, seek out fresh young specimens. As mushrooms age or become waterlogged, they all begin to look alike, rendering accurate identification far more difficult.

If you're identifying your finds in the field, clean them before bringing them back. Brush the dirt off or use a knife to peel off the stuff you don't want. You'll save yourself a lot of effort later.

Trimming your mushrooms in the field will save time and effort later. CREDIT: JACOB RONDER

The results of a successful foray. CREDIT: JAMES CHELIN

Especially if you're not in great physical condition, remember that you have to hike back to your vehicle and you've probably picked up extra mushroom weight to carry back. If you hit the mother lode, that could be a lot of extra weight. Sharing the finds among your group will help reduce your load. Another tip is to consider hiking uphill on the way to your foraging destination. Then you get to hike downhill with your extra weight to get back.

If you find the mother lode, remember that you also will have to do something with all those mushrooms when you get back. If you don't have the facilities back home to handle that much, giving the extra away is a friendly way to solve that problem.

Equipment for Mushroom Hunting
You will need something to carry everything else in, including your mushrooms. Lots of different things get used for this such as picnic baskets, shopping baskets, buckets, shopping bags, backpacks, and mesh bags. Each has its advantages and disadvantages, and you should get whatever works for you.

You should have something to put your mushrooms into. Just tossing them in a pile in your carrying container is not a good idea. Some mushrooms are

Each person has their own set of equipment they take into the field.

fragile and will be crushed by the others. The most common things for edible mushrooms are waxed paper bags, aluminum foil, brown paper lunch bags, and sheets of waxed paper. Plastic bags should not be used, as the mushrooms in them will sweat, and the extra moisture promotes the growth of bacteria, which can lead to food poisoning.

A knife is an important tool for cleaning mushrooms by cutting off the dirty bits and slicing them open to make sure that the insects didn't get to them before you did.

Some sort of tool for digging the base of your mushrooms out of the ground is also important to bring. Many people just use their knives, but gardening tools are also useful.

Bring something to carry your mushrooms in.

Often neglected, bring along something to keep yourself hydrated. In Colorado's dry climate you can lose quite a bit of water while hiking, and a pint or two of some appropriate beverage will help make your foray more pleasant.

Insect repellent can be essential in some areas. Ticks, mosquitoes, and biting flies can be more than just a nuisance. Use whatever seems to work for you.

A camera is a great idea. The camera in your smartphone is fine. Not only does a camera provide you with fun photos of your find and whatever else you might decide to photograph, in future years you can use your photos to remind yourself that those mushrooms grow in those places around those dates.

Some sort of rain gear can be desirable, as you never know if that little rain shower going by might just decide to get big suddenly and drench you. A foldable plastic poncho takes up little space and is lightweight.

Knives are great for digging up the mushroom base and trimming your finds. CREDIT: ALEX MERRYMAN

Setting out. CREDIT: IKUKO LUBOW

Wearing a hat with a brim can be useful. Aside from protecting you from the sun and some rain, it can also protect your face and eyes if you become overly focused on keeping your eyes on the ground while walking.

Something like a GPS device might be valuable to help keep you from getting lost in the woods. If you're the sort that gets lost, consider purchasing a fishing license. Included in the cost of that license is payment for search and rescue teams if they need to go out and find you. Another use for GPS is to record the exact location of productive foraging sites. One reason is that it's difficult to describe to fellow foragers the exact location of a site that's in a nondescript area well off the beaten path. Because the greatest part of the fungal organism is underground, mushrooms of a particular species will generally reappear at the exact same location year after year. But next year, you may not remember precisely where you found that gourmet mother lode 12 months ago.

Beyond those things, it depends on how much stuff you want to carry and how adventurous you are. The farther you hike and the rougher the terrain the more likely that you might want to bring along some sort of survival gear, just in case. Some items for this might include water filters, survival blankets, ropes or paracord, and fire-starting equipment.

Bringing a camera helps you remember even more details. CREDIT: ALEX MERRYMAN

Paper for notes and a tackle box for small mushrooms are often useful. CREDIT: IKUKO LUBOW

Where to Look for Mushrooms

In this part of the country, usually the limiting factor on mushrooms is moisture.

If it's an unusually wet year, mushrooms will be everywhere, including places you might not normally find any. There have been wet years when mushroom hunters have had to clear a space in the midst of huge fruitings of chanterelles to make a place to pitch a tent.

In an average year, mushrooms will concentrate near water sources. Also, in a typical year there will be periods of a week or three when it's wetter than the rest of the season. During and following the wet periods there will be more mushrooms, and they can be found at greater distances from streams.

In a dry year the only places mushrooms will be found will be immediately adjacent to water. During dry spells you will need to expand your

A spruce and subalpine fir forest.

hunting territories to find more places that still have some water if you want to find any mushrooms.

Another handy tip is that the same mushrooms will tend to come up in roughly the same places at about the same time every year. Remember your camera and use it to document when and where you found what so that you can come back in the future and find more.

Mushroom Season

This region has two mushroom seasons each year.

Along the plains at the base of the foothills, the spring season usually begins around late April, peaks around mid- to late May, and tapers off in June. As the weeks pass, the peak spring season will move up in altitude into the mountains and at the higher altitudes will peak around late June. The spring season is when most mushroom hunters focus on morels and oyster mushrooms.

The summer season usually begins in the mountains in mid-July, peaks in early to mid-August, and tapers off from September, ending when it freezes. As the weeks pass, the peak season will move down in altitude, but the peak is generally

A spring morel. CREDIT: MAIA REED

Oyster mushrooms. CREDIT: MAIA REED

still in mid- to late August. The summer season is typically much more fruitful in how many mushrooms are produced, and most of the popular edible species that aren't found in spring are found during this time.

Some Other Notes

The taxonomy of fungi has constantly been changing as a result of rapid advances in molecular biology. As a result, the names of many species are being revised faster than field guides can keep up with the changes. Recent advances in molecular analysis often show that what we once believed to be one species may actually be several different species with very similar mor-

The fruits of success. CREDIT: JACOB RONDER

phology. Or the new research sometimes shows that what we believed to be several different species are actually the same at the molecular level.

The entire situation can be extremely confusing and annoying for non-scientists who are trying to get the identification, taxonomy, and names of mushrooms right.

Despite our best efforts to get the names and classification for mushrooms in this book correct, inevitably the latest molecular research will lead to further revisions before the ink on these pages is dry. Anyone dealing with the description, classification, and nomenclature of fungi must be aware of this flux and alert to the use of both older names and this morning's revisions.

Whenever you see a name followed by the word "group" or "complex," what is meant is that a single name has been used but we now know that there is more than one species that looks like that, and research is under way to figure out how many there are and how to tell them apart.

The phrase "sensu lato" means basically "in a broad sense," and it's usually used to indicate a larger group than the name is now used for. This commonly happens when a genus is split into multiple genera by researchers, and instead we want to refer to the group before it was split up.

Rules for Eating Wild Mushrooms

These are some basic rules to help keep you safe when eating wild mushrooms:

1. **If in doubt, throw it out!** If there is any doubt in your mind that the mushroom you're thinking of eating is edible, then don't eat it. Remember that if you eat the wrong mushroom you will get sick and could possibly die. The most common cause of poisoning is misidentification. If you're not sure, save the collection and show it to somebody that knows what they're doing. You will find more mushrooms in the future, and you don't have to rush into eating some mushrooms.

   The good news is that there are only a handful of species that are known to be lethal among the many thousand you may encounter. If you're careful, it's extremely unlikely that these few killers will sneak into your food chain. (Most of the mushroom poisonings in America have occurred among immigrants who mistook a toxic species here for an extremely similar edible mushroom in their homeland.)

   However, the bad news is that there are quite a few more mushrooms out there that won't kill you but will temporarily make you wish you were dead. One author calls them the lose-your-lunch bunch.

2. Never eat a rotting or maggot-infested mushroom. As you find your mushrooms, cut them open to be sure that you beat the insects to them. Most of our edible mushrooms are also an important part of the diet of many kinds of insects. If you cut your mushroom in half and find lots of tunnels inside, those tunnels are made by insect larvae burrowing through the flesh of the mushroom and eating it. While the insect larvae themselves are actually nutritious, the wastes they leave behind in the tunnels are not.

3. Watch for potential environmental contamination. There are a lot of old mines scattered throughout Colorado, and the mine tailings are often a source of toxic metals such as lead and arsenic. Mushrooms growing near tailings

are likely to be contaminated with those metals and can poison you even if the mushroom is an edible species.

Another source of external toxins are various chemicals that are sprayed on plants. Golf courses look so pristine because they spray weed killers to get rid of everything but that nice grass. Sometimes weed killers will be sprayed near roadsides to clear them of excess vegetation.

Note the lack of holes inside the bases of these trimmed mushrooms. CREDIT: JACOB RONDER

4. Unless you specifically know otherwise, cook your mushrooms. Many edible mushrooms are poisonous raw, for example, honey mushrooms and morels.

5. Avoid overeating. Mushrooms should be consumed in moderation. Eating too much of anything will make you sick, and mushrooms are not an exception.

6. The first time you eat a new species of mushroom, eat only a small amount and keep some uncooked in the refrigerator. If you get sick later, the uncooked bit will be important.

7. Especially if you're serving mushrooms to others, get two independent opinions. Many mycological groups around the country adhere to a two-person rule. No mushroom goes into the community pot until TWO knowledgeable people acting independently agree that it is safe to consume.

8. Wash everything really well. Then wash it again.

9. If you get sick, **seek medical attention!** With even the deadliest mushrooms your odds of survival are over 90% if you have prompt medical treatment.

If you are sick enough to go to the emergency room, bring your uncooked mushrooms with you. The mushrooms can be identified to help determine your treatment. It is very possible that your mushrooms are edible, and your illness is due to something else.

If you aren't quite sick enough to head for a hospital, consider calling the Rocky Mountain Poison Center. The call is free, they will answer 24 hours a day, and the doctors, nurses, and pharmacists that work there can contact people to help identify your mushrooms and advise you on what to do.

The phone number for the Rocky Mountain Poison Center is:

1-800-222-1222

Trees
by Orion Aon

Trees and mushrooms are deeply connected, often contributing to each other's survival. Mycorrhizal mushrooms rely on trees for nutrients, and in turn, they provide the tree with methods of gathering resources that would otherwise be unavailable to its root system. Saprotrophic mushrooms decompose the dead and dying debris and keep the forest from being overwhelmed with organic material. The only mushrooms that don't aid the forests are the parasites that attack and kill trees for their gain. There is balance, but parasitic fungi can easily exploit forests weakened by drought, insects, or other environmental stressors.

Knowing at least the basics of tree identification in your area can drastically improve your abilities as a mushroom forager. The best mushroom hunters are also some of the better tree identifiers. Knowing your trees means that you can quickly tell if a forest would be a suitable habitat for that mycorrhizal species you're after, or if you're on the correct aspect of the mountain, and even if you're in the right elevation range. As an example, a ponderosa pine forest would not be the right habitat to look for porcini or matsutake but would be excellent for lobster mushrooms. The same goes for a spruce forest when looking for oyster mushrooms since they rarely fruit from dead conifers. However, spruce forests are the prime habitat for many of the other edible mushrooms foragers are targeting.

In the southern Rocky Mountains, we have several different forest types, from the lowest elevation riparian areas dominated by cottonwoods, willows,

A subalpine spruce/fir forest with mountain marigold in bloom.

and other deciduous species, to our highest elevation spruce/fir forests and even micro-forests in the alpine zone made of dwarf trees, called krummholz. The riparian, aspen, and major coniferous groups are the most important forest types to learn for mushroom hunting.

The lower and middle elevation riparian habitats are home to various deciduous species, including cottonwood, willow, elm, ash, boxelder, birch, alder, and several fruiting species such as plum, cherry, hawthorn, and apple. The main mushrooms found in these habits are oysters, morels, ink caps, and maybe even the rare-to-this-region lion's mane.

Above the riparian habitats, the following essential forest types to learn are stands dominated by ponderosa pines. Ponderosa forests in this region are home to the coveted lobster mushroom and can also harbor chanterelles, shrimp Russula, Agaricus, edible Amanita, some puffballs, and the white king bolete. A true cornucopia when they get enough rain for the mushrooms to fruit!

Next are the pure stands of quaking aspen, the main deciduous or hardwood tree that dominates this region's mountain habitats. Because aspens are one of the only non-conifer species in these habitats, they are home to some unique edible mushrooms, including aspen oysters and wild enoki!

Lodgepole pine forests are the last pure forest type found in this region and are one of the most common. Lodgepole pines are a favorite of the western matsutake and can also contain chanterelles, corals, and slippery jacks.

Aspen forest. CREDIT: IKUKO LUBOW

Lodgepole pine forest.

A nice king bolete in a spruce/fir subalpine forest.

At the highest elevations, we have spruce/fir forests. Engelmann spruce and subalpine fir comprise most of these forests. However, they can also include blue spruce and white fir. These forests are prime for many delicious mushroom species, including king boletes, milk caps, chanterelles, Agaricus, hedgehogs, jellies, and many others!

Finally, bringing together pieces of all of the previous forests, we have mixed-conifer forests. These are found throughout this region's middle and high elevations and include many of the above species as well as Douglas fir, limber pine, and bristlecone pine. The large variety of tree species makes these forests home to many of the delectable mushrooms already listed!

Other forest types that may not be as crucial for mushroom hunting include piñon-juniper, oak shrubland, and the alpine krummholz. Additionally, we have a variety of grass and shrublands environments that can also be home to edible mushroom species. These habitats will mainly house the saprotrophic species such as puffballs, ink caps, and Agaricus.

Knowing your trees is like a superpower when it comes to mushroom hunting. So while you're foraging, don't forget to look up and give recognition to the trees. Without them, many of our favorite mushrooms wouldn't be there for us to pick and eat.

1. Chanterelles

A bountiful pick of chanterelles. CREDIT: JENNIFER BELL

by Alex Merryman

The chanterelles are some of the best-loved of the edible mushrooms. Although covered together in this chapter, this is a group of very distantly related mushrooms having the similar feature of shallow "gills" (also called "false gills") that are more ridge-like and veined to completely smooth, as distinct from the typical flat plate-like gills of most mushrooms. They are very popular edibles around the world, with their lovely fruity aromas and mild taste. We have only a few representatives in our region, while on the West Coast and farther east there are many more species.

Chanterelle. If we have a wet summer, these will be growing everywhere! CREDIT: IKUKO LUBOW

RAINBOW CHANTERELLE
Cantharellus roseocanus

Family: Cantharellaceae

Ecology: Summer and fall, associated with conifers (especially Engelmann spruce and lodgepole pine), usually above 8,000 feet, in or near the edges of forests, often growing with moss/grass in slightly rocky terrain, and often scattered to gregarious. It is a terrestrial mushroom (grows directly from the soil, not from wood).

Description: *Cantharellus* have distinct ridge-like spore-bearing surfaces that run down the stem (decurrent). They tend to be triangular to somewhat funnel-shaped in cross-section, and the cap margins are irregular or wavy. It is not uncommon to find several fruit bodies which have fused together. The stem and spore surface can be a brilliant yellow-orange, while the cap is often a duller yellow to buff color. Key identifying features of *C. roseocanus* are its beautiful, sweet, fruitlike aroma many compare to the scent of apricots; pure white flesh; and the ability to pull the mushroom apart like string cheese.

Edibility: Edible and excellent.

False Chanterelle. Notice the difference between these gills and the ridges on a true chanterelle.

Notes: There is a very similar mushroom, the false chanterelle, *Hygrophoropsis aurantiacum*, that is common. False chanterelles grow from dead wood, although the wood can be buried, and they are thinner fleshed. The gills on false chanterelles are true gills rather than the much thicker ridges on true chanterelles.

Pig's Ear. These are usually found in wet areas. CREDIT: IAN FIERMAN

PIG'S EAR
Gomphus clavatus

Family: Gomphaceae
Ecology: Summer and fall, associated with conifers (especially spruces and firs), usually above 8,000 feet.
Description: *Gomphus* has an indistinct cap; rather the entire fruiting body is somewhat tubular or club-like with no distinct stem. They are orange or lilac to brown/buff in color. Well-defined wrinkles/folds typically run the length of the fruit body, and the cap itself is generally smooth and irregularly shaped.
Edibility: Edible, though some have reported gastric distress.

The underside is typical of most chanterelles, except purple. CREDIT: GINGER McKEY

Blue Chanterelle. Although lacking flavor, they will dye the foods they are cooked with so you can actually have green eggs with your ham! CREDIT: JOSEPH O'HALLARON

BLUE CHANTERELLE
Polyozellus atrolazulinus

Family: Thelephoraceae

Ecology: Summer and fall, associated with conifers (especially spruces and firs), usually above 8,000 feet, in conifer forests, among moss, often scattered to gregarious.

Description: *Polyozellus* forms large fused clusters of intensely violet to inky black fan- or trumpet-shaped fruit bodies with a wrinkled to smooth spore-bearing surface. The spore-bearing underside can be brilliant indigo blue to black in color. Occasionally the underside can appear whitish/grayish in some areas. The fruit bodies are densely clustered, and rather brittle—they can break off from the cluster without much effort.

Edibility: Edible, though somewhat lacking in flavor.

RECIPE

Chanterelles over Baguette

BY JAMES CHELIN

Time: About 20 minutes

Serves: 4 to 5 people

Ingredients
A handful of chanterelles (golden or blue)
1 French baguette
Arugula (I get mine from the garden; optional)
Goat cheese log or crumbled (omit for vegan friendly)
Butter (switch to olive or coconut oil for vegan friendly)
1 garlic clove
Sea salt to taste

Preparation
1. Clean your mushrooms to remove any dirt.
2. Slice and saute with butter and minced garlic until cooked.
3. Salt to taste.
4. Slice your baguette and arrange on a plate.
5. Top with arugula, mushrooms, and goat cheese.
6. Serve with your favorite wine.

It's really that simple! The truth is you can use many different mushrooms in the same way. If you prefer your baguette toasted you can do that too! I often do this with a camp stove out in the woods at the end of a foray because it's easy, fun, and a fantastic way to end the day.

Blue chanterelles over baguette. CREDIT: JAMES CHELIN

RECIPE

Chanterelle and Corn Salsa

BY IKUKO LUBOW

Ingredients
½ cup chanterelles chopped
2 ears corn
½ cup sweet onion chopped
2 small jalapeno peppers chopped
1 lime
Salt to taste
¼ cup cilantro minced

Preparation
1. Cut the kernels off the ears of corn. If you haven't done this before, just use a knife and slice along the length of the ears. It's pretty easy to do.
2. Roast the corn and onions.
3. Add sweet red peppers or fresh peaches (optional).
4. Let it cool; then add jalapeno peppers and cilantro.
5. Squeeze juice of lime over and mix well.

2. Boletes

Boletes emerging from the earth. CREDIT: JACOB RONDER

by Roy Halling

The boletes in the porcini group (Boletaceae) are some of the most desirable edible mushrooms. The Suillaceae is related to the porcinis but has a different evolutionary history. While some are edible, they aren't as highly prized. Nearly all boletes have a sponge-like underside (tubes) and can be fairly common in conifer forests and aspen groves of the Rockies. Because of their size and colors, they are highly visible, but the diversity is much higher on the West Coast and in the eastern United States where oaks are more common. The boletes in both families form obligate associations with tree roots (mycorrhizae).

Boletes collected among the aspens. CREDIT: JACOB RONDER

King Bolete, *Boletus rubriceps*. This is probably the most sought after mushroom in the Rockies.

KING BOLETE, RUBY PORCINI, STEINPILZ, CÉP
Boletus rubriceps

Family: Boletaceae

Ecology: July to September, associated with conifers, especially spruce, often solitary or scattered.

Description: Cap medium to large, usually dry but sometimes slightly sticky to greasy in wet weather, round at first then flattened with age. The color is dark brownish red at first, but can fade a little with age. The interior is typically quite firm when young, white, does not change color when exposed, but can be infested with insect larvae. The underside is sponge-like with the tubes white at first becoming olive-yellow with age and are spongy. The robust stalk is white or light brownish red and has a fine, raised network on the surface. Odor and taste are mild.

Edibility: Edible and excellent.

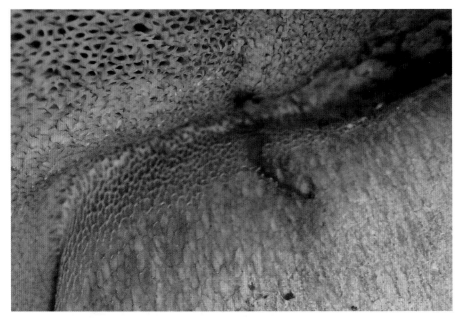

Note the netlike pattern of ridges at the top of the stem.

People finding these always seem to be happy about it.

Boletus barrowsii. These are most commonly found under ponderosa pine and douglas fir.
CREDIT: IKUKO LUBOW

WHITE KING BOLETE
Boletus barrowsii

Family: Boletaceae
Ecology: Late June through August, mycorrhizal with a mixture of conifers, most often pine, often solitary but sometimes scattered about.
Description: Caps medium to very large, dry, white to off-white, sometimes with a hint of grayish tan, round at first then flattened with age. The interior is white and firm when young, doesn't change color when exposed, but once in a while will have insect larvae infestations with age. The tubes are white when young and become olive yellowish and spongy with age. The stalk is robust and can be quite broad near the base, with coloring similar to the cap, and with a raised white to pale tan network veining especially near the upper parts. Taste is mild and the odor is mild and can sometimes be slightly fragrant.
Edibility: Edible and excellent.

Suillus lakei. The scaly cap and ring on the stem help separate these from other Suillus. CREDIT: ALEX MERRYMAN

LAKE'S BOLETE, WESTERN PAINTED SUILLUS
Suillus lakei

Family: Suillaceae

Ecology: Appearing in late summer to the early fall in conifer forests *specifically* associated with Douglas fir. Can be clustered or appearing singly.

Description: Caps small to medium, usually dry, but often slightly sticky, with finely tufted scales, often appressed with age, dull red to reddish brown at first, soon fading with age, with some pale yellow showing between the scales. Flesh is pale yellow when fresh and becomes a pinkish red when exposed to air. A whitish veil covers the yellow tubes when young and collapses with age, leaving some fibrils hanging from the cap edge and forming a distinct zone near the upper part of the stalk. The tubes are shallow, staining pinkish brown when bruised; angular; and radially oriented. The stalk is yellow above the whitish veil zone, reddish brown below with some fine scattered scales, and white at the base. It has a mild odor and taste.

Edibility: While the taste is mild, the texture can be a little fibrous, especially in the stalk.

Suillus brevipes. Probably the best of the Suillus, the flavor is better if they are dried. CREDIT: ROY HALLING

SHORT-STALKED SLIPPERY JACK
Suillus brevipes

Family: Suillaceae

Ecology: Appearing July through September, in conifer forests, particularly with lodgepole pine.

Description: Caps medium-sized, round to flattened, sticky with a jelly-like substance on the surface, dark brown to red-brown to yellow-brown, smooth and shiny in dry weather and the skin surface peels off. Flesh is white and firm at first, becomes a dull pale yellow when old, and does not change color when exposed. The tubes are pale yellow at first and a dull olive-yellow with age. Stalk is short and stubby, dry and smooth to the naked eye, white at first but becomes yellowish with age. Odor is mild and the taste likewise, but can become a bit acidic.

Edibility: Edible if properly prepared and the skin is removed from the cap.

Suillus tomentosus. Sometimes the color can cause you to think someone has thrown away an orange peel. CREDIT: JOSEPH O'HALLARON

BLUE-STAINING SLIPPERY JACK
Suillus tomentosus

Family: Suillaceae

Ecology: July to early September, in conifer forests, usually with lodgepole pine.

Description: Caps small to medium size, round to flattened, sticky, with a matted coating of soft hairs at first, and these sometimes hanging from the edge, then with scattered, appressed, fine scales and eventually almost completely smooth; the scales grayish to ocher-yellow or olive-yellow to reddish brown on top of an orange-yellow background. Flesh is yellow and shows a pale blue reaction when exposed to the air. Tubes are very fine and angular, light brown to pale cinnamon brown, sometimes exuding delicate yellow moisture droplets, changing to light blue when bruised. Stalk mostly cylindrical or slightly enlarged downward, dry to moist, yellowish to orange-yellow with darker orange to pale brown gland-like dots, white at the base. Odor and taste are mild to not distinctive.

Edibility: Poor quality.

Leccinum insigne. Although many eat these, too many people end up in the emergency room after eating them, so please don't. CREDIT: ALEXIS MURRAY

ASPEN ORANGE CAP, SCABER STALK
Leccinum insigne

Family: Boletaceae

Ecology: Appearing in late June through September and only associated with aspen trees, often near the edge of groves of the tree.

Description: Caps small to large, round to flattened, dry when young and fresh, but sometimes slightly sticky with age or in wet weather, usually somewhat velvety at first, orange to brownish orange, with a sterile flap hanging from the edge when young. Flesh is white, but will slowly turn a purplish gray to nearly black when exposed. Tubes are a pale yellow at first, becoming a light brown to pinkish gray and becoming a pale grayish brown when bruised. Stalk is slightly broader at the base and can become quite long with age compared to the cap width; covered with short, white to gray, scale-like tufts (scabers) when young

Leccinum fibrillosum. More reddish brown cap and associated only with conifers. Characteristic sterile flap on the cap edge and black scabers on the stalk. CREDIT: ROY HALLING

that become dark brown to black with maturity. The base of the stalk can often bruise blue-green on the outside and inside.

Edibility: DO NOT EAT. Even though the odor and a brief taste are mild to pleasant, many people have experienced gastric upset and hospitalization, especially if older material is eaten and/or if not thoroughly cooked.

Notes: There are other boletes of the scaber stalk group in the Rocky Mountains with more reddish-brown caps and some have a flesh that changes to a dull pink color before changing over to dark gray. The species with orange- to red-brown-colored caps will have a sterile flap around the edge when young. Also, the density of the scabers on the stalk is variable but they can be quite tightly packed together. The large majority of these boletes are associated only with aspen, but there is at least one known to occur only with conifers. If there is a Scaber Stalk occurring with a non-native cultivated birch, those species often have an off-white to dark gray color on the cap surface.

RECIPE

Beef and Barley Soup with Boletes

BY IKUKO LUBOW

Ingredients
6 quarts water or beef broth
1 pound beef boneless spare ribs
1 pound beef soup bones
1 cup onion
½ cup barley
½ to 1 pound boletes fresh or 1 ounce reconstituted

Preparation
1. If using dried mushrooms, soak them in warm water for 20 minutes before using.
2. Place ribs and soup bones in a pressure cooker and cook for 30 minutes to an hour until meat is tender. Remove the bones.
3. Add barley and onion and cook additional 30 minutes.
4. Add salt to taste.

RECIPE

Boletes in White Sauce

BY ED LUBOW

Ingredients
1 pound fresh boletes, cut into bite-sized pieces
3 tablespoons butter
3 tablespoons butter (yes, a second bit of butter)
3 tablespoons flour
1 egg yolk
1 cup half-and-half
Lemon juice to taste
Salt and pepper to taste

Preparation
1. Saute the boletes in 3 tablespoons butter. Remove the cooked mushrooms and reserve the liquid.
2. Melt 3 tablespoons butter in a non-stick pan; then add the flour, stirring to avoid lumps until thickened.
3. Add water to the reserved liquid from the first step to make 1 cup. Add to the sauteed flour.
4. Beat the egg yolk and blend with the half-and-half. Add to the sauce mixture.
5. Add the cooked mushrooms to the mixture, stirring well.
6. Add salt, pepper, and lemon juice to taste.

This sauce is great over meats, vegetables, or even toast or rice.

3. Morels and Other Ascomycetes

Morels are some of the most popular edible mushrooms. CREDIT: MAIA REED

by Trent Blizzard

Morels are among the most sought after and elusive mushrooms in Colorado. Colorado has five types of distinct morels for enthusiasts to hunt: natural yellows, natural blacks, burn morels, landscape morels, and half-free morels. Morels are both mysterious and unpredictable; the habitat, tree associations, elevations and seasons are best estimates and certainly outliers are possible and probably common.

The morel lifestyle is also mysterious. It is likely they are mycorrhizal during certain stages of their life, living within the forest floor and enjoying a harmonious relationship with their trees. Also likely, they may convert into a saprobic fungus during their lifespan, as evident by their abundant growth around dead and dying trees.

All morels can be discerned by a few key identification rules:
1. The cap base is fused to the stem (except half-free morels).
2. The cap and stem are hollow.

"White Morel." No, this is not a morel. Notice the spongy look of the stem. This is a stinkhorn with the dark slime washed off from the cap. We get asked about "White Morels" every year. CREDIT: IKUKO LUBOW

False Morel. Notice that the cap is wrinkled instead of being pits and ridges. CREDIT: IKUKO LUBOW

A nice batch of yellow morels.

NATURAL MORELS

Natural morels occur year after year in the same spots, weather conditions permitting. They follow specific seasons and are found in specific habitats. Yet, they are elusive and have frustrated many local foragers. Not only are morels rare, they require two things:

1. Warm spring weather. Spring fever causes many foragers to go out searching too early in the spring and they don't find morels. A certain amount of warming is really necessary for these naturals to fruit, and the early hunter never finds them. In Colorado, that often means mid to late April is the likely time to start finding them on the front range.
2. Rain. Morels are highly moisture dependent. They require a 2- to 6-week pattern of regular rainy weather to actualize into edible fruits. In reality, this probably means a little more rain than average to trigger good fruitings.

Black Morel. CREDIT: RON WOLF

NATURAL YELLOW MORELS

These are the first naturals that occur in Colorado foraging season. They are most common in riparian habitats and are typically associated with cottonwood, but not exclusively. The yellow morel's elevation range is approximately 5,500 to 7,500 feet, and they move up in elevation from April through May. Typically they are found in grassy riparian habitats, especially around dying or distressed cottonwood trees. They are often difficult to spot, hidden in grass and dense forest litter. Look for them as the cottonwoods start leafing out, concurrent with feral asparagus and when the grass is close to ankle to knee high. These lower-elevation morels fruit 60–90 days after the snow has melted in these areas, so rain is needed between snowmelt and yellow morel fruitings.

Yellow Morels. This is the morel that grows along creeks and rivers on the plains in April and May.

YELLOW MOREL
Morchella americana

Family: Morchellaceae

Description: Medium to large mushrooms with a roughly conic or egg-shaped cap that is yellowish and consists of pits with ridges between them. The cap is attached to the stem at the base of the cap, not the top, as with other mushrooms. The stem is white and more or less cylindrical. The entire mushroom is hollow.

Edibility: Delish and gourmet. Must be cooked before eaten; poisonous if eaten raw. Preserves well by dehydration, can also be frozen.

Notes: Previously known as *Morchella esculenta* and found from the Rockies and to the east, including Arizona and Utah. Grows single, scattered, or clustered. The ridges on its pits are a lighter color than the pits themselves. Check the inside of the mushroom before cooking, as slugs can commonly be found to have made their way inside.

NATURAL BLACK MORELS

The black morels start fruiting as the yellow finishes. Most commonly, they are found in both aspen and conifer forests and also mixed forests (aspen and conifer) from 7,000 to 9,000 feet, moving upward from mid-May through June. They are not exclusive to one conifer type, but do not grow in recently burned forests. These forests are usually a moist environment, staying wet as the snowmelt soaks the ground. Still, some rain after snowmelt is very helpful. Also, some warm days and nights help encourage fruiting. Look for aspen trees that have small nickel-sized leaves and you will know the seasonal timing is right. Also, look for forests with distressed and dying trees, especially aspen. Like most morels, these tend to fruit more when their host trees are stressed or dying. Indeed, like many morels, they probably enjoy a mycorrhizal relationship with a living tree that turns into a saprobic relationship when the tree perishes. The black morel is hard to spot, but, once you find one there are certain to be more nearby, so mark the spot; like the yellow morels, that patch might fruit every year if the conditions are right.

Black Morel. This is the most common morel in the mountain areas in spring and early summer.

BLACK MOREL
Morchella brunnea

Family: Morchellaceae

Description: Small to medium (rarely large) mushrooms with a roughly conic or egg-shaped cap that is dark brown and consists of pits with ridges between them. The cap is attached to the stem at the base of the cap, not the top, as with other mushrooms. The stem is white and more or less cylindrical. The entire mushroom is hollow.

Edibility: Delish and gourmet. Must be cooked before eaten; poisonous if eaten raw. Preserves well by dehydration, can also be frozen.

Similar Species: It is likely other black morel species grow in Colorado. *Morchella snyderi*, commonly associated with Douglas firs (and lower elevations: 6,000–8,000 feet), is a possible find.

Notes: Grows in the western United States and is similar to *M. angusticeps* of the eastern United States. Features dark ridges and a relatively smooth stem. Grows single, scattered, or clustered. The ridges on its pits are a lighter color than the pits themselves.

Most of the time morels are found singly, not in clusters.
CREDIT: IKUKO LUBOW

BURN MORELS

Burn morels are the other type of morels, and are not considered "naturals" because they require a special post–forest fire habitat to fruit. However, while they are in the black morel group, they are usually a unique species that only fruits in the year or two after a forest fire.

Burn morels *always* associate with conifer trees. That means they can be found with trees like ponderosa pine, lodgepole pine, Douglas fir, subalpine fir, or Engelmann spruce. However, the most abundant and regular fruitings tend to occur in the fir/spruce forests that begin to dominate from 9,000–11,000 feet.

Typically these higher elevation locations don't start warming up enough until mid-June. However, the good news is that the burn morels will fruit in waves, going up above 10,000 feet in August and September in a good year with spring rains and summer monsoon weather patterns. They tend to be more productive in shady areas, so look for burned forest that still has some canopy coverage. They also like it when the ground is covered in brown needles and duff (vs. bare ash), which creates a moister micro-climate for the baby fruiting morels.

There are several species of morels that can be found within burn perimeters, explaining why they fruit in waves. Likely, these species include *M. sextelata*, *M. eximia*, *M. exuberans,* and *M. tomentosa*. And maybe more! While they can be difficult to ID it the species without a microscope or DNA test, the marquee species is *M. tomentosa*, or gray morel.

Reference: Blizzard, ModernForager.com

Gray Morel. Large fruitings of these have been found in August and September. CREDIT: GINGER McKEY

GRAY MOREL, FUZZY FOOT, BLACK FOOT
Morchella tomentosa

Description: Medium to large mushrooms with a roughly conic or egg-shaped cap that is grayish to dark brownish and consists of pits with finely fuzzy ridges between them. The cap is attached to the stem at the base of the cap, not the top, as with other mushrooms. The stem is white and more or less cylindrical. The entire mushroom is hollow.

Edibility: Delish and gourmet. Thicker and heavier than other morel species. Must be cooked before eaten; poisonous if eaten raw. Burn morels are best when collected clean, to avoid ashy flavors. Preserves well by dehydration, can also be frozen.

Similar Species: This mushroom is unique to burns; however, it can get quite a yellowish pale when older, which creates confusion.

Notes: Typically dark and covered with velvety fuzz on the cap ridges and stem when young. The tiny hairs disappear to the naked eye as the mushroom matures. This species usually lightens with age, but the color can be all over the board from young to old and a wide variety is typically found.

LANDSCAPE MORELS

These elusive morels will pop up, seemingly randomly and mysteriously, in wood chips and bark used for landscaping. Possibly *M. rufobrunnea* or *M. importuna*.

HALF-FREE MORELS

The half-free morel is technically a morel, but is smaller and more fragile than the other Colorado morels. They fruit sporadically and unpredictably in the same riparian habitat as yellow morels and typically concurrently.

Typical Landscape morels. The Morel species can be tough to tell apart, but all are choice edibles.
CREDIT: JOSEPH O'HALLARON

HALF-FREE MOREL, PECKERHEAD
Morchella punctipes and *M. populiphila*

Description: Grow alone or scattered. Unusual for morels, the stem is attached to the cap with the margin of the cap clearly overhanging the stem. Slight in stature.
Edibility: Delicious but slighter in stature than most other morels.
Similar Species: This mushroom is unique to burns; however, it can get quite a yellowish pale when older, which creates confusion.

Lobster Mushroom. One of the easiest mushrooms to identify, and an excellent edible. CREDIT: ORION AON

LOBSTER MUSHROOM
Hypomyces lactifluorum
by Joe O'Hallaron

Family: Hypocreaceae

Ecology: Found fruiting in summer and fall at lower elevations, associated most often with ponderosa pine, growing solitary or gregariously, often under layers of pine duff.

Description: *H. lactifluorum* is not your typical mushroom, but rather an ascomycete fungus that parasitizes the fruiting bodies of Russula and Lactarius species. Over time it transforms the entire surface of the host mushroom into a bright orange color, even covering and smoothing over the gills. Fruiting bodies are medium to large and the flesh inside is white. Unlike the crumbly or grainy texture of the host species, the flesh becomes denser and firm after full parasitization. It is most frequently reported as parasitizing *Russula brevipes*, though the host species can be difficult to identify.

Edibility: Excellent edible.

RECIPE

Manitou Springs' Spring Morel Pasta

BY JENNIFER BELL

Ingredients

6 fresh morels or 6 dried morels soaked in hot broth or hot water

Slivers of garlic, or chopped shallots or diced sweet onion, or all three

¼ pound chunked-up guanciale (bacon is too strong a flavor for this delicate dish)

½ pound linguine

½ pint heavy cream

⅓ cup medium sherry

⅓ cup cooked light-colored legume like chickpeas or lima beans

10 ounces fresh English peas

1 tablespoon Italian parsley

Parmesan or Romano cheese

Extra virgin olive oil

Salt and pepper

Preparation

1. As the morels soak (if dry), place a large pot of salted water on the stove to boil for the pasta.
2. Heat a 10-inch saute pan and then add a glug of extra virgin olive oil. Place the guanciale chunks in the pan till they get crispy and then set aside. Throw the onion in the pan and cook on medium low till transparent.
3. Toss your pasta in the boiling water for 8 to 10 minutes. When the noodles are almost al dente put the peas in the water for no more than 90 seconds. Strain them and add a little more oil or butter as they cool.
4. Deglaze the saute pan with the sherry on a high flame. Add fresh ground pepper and as much salt as you like. Return the guanciale to the pan; then finish with cream and your morels.
5. Unite the pasta with the sauce and serve with chopped parsley and grated cheese.

A very cold sauvignon blanc would be the ideal companion to this dish.

4. Puffballs

Puffballs are solid and white inside when they are edible. CREDIT: IKUKO LUBOW

by Ian Fierman

The "Puffballs" cover a vast group of fungi from several different genera and families within the order of Agaricales. They are a form of basidiomycete with spores which are essentially trapped inside of the fruiting body, forming what is called a gleba. The method of releasing these spores is in turn different than other mushrooms, in that the mushroom must age to a point of decomposition where the outer skin is brittle enough to burst and the spores are then released, often ejecting large and impressive greenish-brown clouds into the air, particularly when agitated by a strong wind or a tromping animal. They are generally somewhere in the range of white to tan or brownish in color but vary greatly in size from less than a couple of inches across in smaller species like *Lycoperdon perlatum*, to over two feet in cases like the giant western puffball, *Calvatia booniana*.

Sometimes, puffballs are lumped under the name "Gasteromycetes" (gasteroid fungi), which is a term representing a number of unrelated orders of mushrooms that are all alike in having similar modes of sporulation as described above.

The rule to follow regarding edibility with all puffballs is to cut the mushroom open and observe the interior flesh; if the spores (gleba) on the inside display any color other than white in a cross-section, then you could have a puffball that has started to sporulate, or you may have stumbled upon a Scleroderma (purplish-black interior). Puffballs at this stage are considered old and inedible; Scleroderma are toxic. This issue is easily avoided by never consuming anything that looks like a puffball but lacks the completely white interior flesh. Sometimes, unopened Amanita buttons, with their cottony white universal veils, can superficially resemble small puffballs, which is why the method of cutting a cross-section through the mushroom is important here too, because there will always be some visible gilled mushroom forming inside of the "egg" of an Amanita as opposed to being solid throughout.

Historically, puffballs have many uses. They are a good food source, and depending on the size of the specimen, a single mushroom can reap a large

The bigger puffballs can easily be volleyball sized or larger. CREDIT: IKUKO LUBOW

This is not a puffball. This is an Amanita button, illustrating why you need to slice your puffballs as well as what you'll see inside.

harvest of many meals for the forager. They are also known to have some practical and medicinal uses, which include but are not limited to burning giant puffballs under the nests of bees in order to sedate them with the smoke and remove the nest safely from areas where they are unwanted, and using the developed green spores from older puffball mushrooms on cuts and even larger wounds to help with the clotting of blood.

In this chapter we will cover some of the species found in the Southern Rocky Mountain region.

This is not a puffball, although it resembles one. Note the thick skin and the dark purplish inside. This is a Scleroderma, and it will make you sick if you eat one. CREDIT: IKUKO LUBOW

Western Giant Puffball. These can easily be mistaken for a volleyball at a distance.

WESTERN GIANT PUFFBALL
Calvatia booniana
by Alex Merryman

Family: Lycoperdaceae

Ecology: Summer and fall, in arid lower elevations or high subalpine meadows. They may grow alone, gregariously, or in large fairy ring formations of many fruit bodies.

Description: The western giant puffball is one of the largest mushrooms found in the South-ern Rockies—specimens up to 2 feet in diameter have been discovered! It is usually 20–50 centimeters (~8–20 inches) in diameter, and may be spherical but is more often oblong/egg-shaped. The mushroom is white or off-white in color, with large scales/warts covering the surface in mature specimens. There is usually no stem to speak of so the mushroom often rests directly on the ground, or it may be attached to its substrate (which can be

You should only eat puffballs that are solid and entirely white inside. CREDIT: IAN FIERMAN

organic material or soil, as the mushroom is both saprobic and terrestrial) by a cord-like feature called a rhizomorph.

Like all puffballs, cutting a fresh western giant puffball open should yield completely uniform white inner flesh, with no immature gills present (although the massive size alone is probably the best identifying characteristic for this particular species). Also, like all puffballs, as the western giant puffball ages, the color of the inner flesh (actually the mushroom's spore mass, or the gleba) changes from white to yellow to brown, and finally disintegrates, releasing the spores within.

Edibility: Edible, but somewhat lacking in flavor. The size and texture of this mushroom lends itself well to recipes as a tofu substitute.

Common Puffball, *Lycoperdon perlatum.* This is the common whitish puffball on the ground in the mountains in summer. CREDIT: GINGER McKEY

COMMON PUFFBALL, GEM-STUDDED PUFFBALL & PEAR-SHAPED PUFFBALL
Lycoperdon perlatum Pers. & *Apioperdon pyriforme*
by Saadia Naiman

Family: Agaricaceae

Ecology: Both species are common, widely distributed, and can be found in late summer through early fall. *A. pyriforme* may also appear in spring or summer. *L. perlatum* usually grows in the soil solitary or in groups or clusters while *A. pyriforme* is one of the only puffballs that exclusively grows on wood in groups and compact clusters.

Description: *L. perlatum* and *A. pyriforme* are similar species with a few key differences. Both species are small to medium in size with *A. pyriforme* being slightly smaller and both exhibiting an inverted pear shape. In fact, pyriform means pear-shaped. Both species have rounded or flat tops with a tapered, wide sterile base. *A. pyriforme* tends to have a more

Pear-Shaped Puffball, *Apioperdon pyriforme*. This common puffball grows only on wood. CREDIT: RON WOLF

pinched base with visible attached threadlike strings (mycelial cords). *L. perlatum* can be easily recognized when young by the large firm conical spines, spikes, studs, and granules on the exterior surface, which eventually fall off, leaving patterned surface scars. In contrast, the outer surface of *A. pyriforme* is smoother with smaller and softer granules that fall off to reveal a smooth surface. The color of *L. perlatum* is white or pale when young whereas *A. pyriforme* tends to be darker, usually light tan to yellow-brown. Overall, both species are firm when young, and as aging progresses, softening happens, darkening occurs, and outer surfaces become smooth with the appearance of a distinct central pore opening on top to facilitate spore dispersal. Interior color of both will be white when young, and with age the color will change from white toward yellow, to green and then to brown. Interior texture will also be firm when young and change with age from soft to mushy, and then finally become a brown powdery spore mass.

Odor is indistinct and taste is mild. In terms of taste, *A. pyriforme* is considered to be better.

Edibility: Edible only at the stage when firm and white inside with a uniform white color throughout.

Notes: Slice in half from top to bottom to ensure that the interior is completely white inside with no sign of a cap, gills, or stalk, which would be an indication of a young Amanita and should NOT be consumed.

Common Puffballs. CREDIT: JACOB RONDER

RECIPE

Puffball Pizza

BY JAMES CHELIN

Time: About 45 minutes

Serves: 3 to 4 people

Ingredients
1 large puffball
Marinara sauce
Olive oil
Sea salt
Parsley, basil, or similar
Mozzarella or vegan cheese
Toppings (optional or get creative!):

Pepperoni (optional)
Agaricus mushrooms
Black olives

Puffball Pizza CREDIT: JAMES CHELIN

Preparation
1. Clean your puffball by washing it quickly with cold water, and then use a paper towel to remove any dirt.
2. Slice into ½-inch-thick slices.
3. Trim the edges especially where still dirty.
4. Brush both sides with olive oil and sprinkle with sea salt.
5. Place the slices on a baking sheet and bake at 450° F for 10–15 minutes, flipping over halfway through cooking.
6. Remove from the oven. Add your sauce, grated cheese, and desired toppings.
7. Sprinkle with a little parsley (optional).
8. Bake for an additional 10 minutes or so.
9. Remove from the oven, let it cool, and enjoy!

5. Polypores

Turkey Tails. They have some of the prettier tops of any mushrooms. CREDIT: RON WOLF

by Michael Heim

Artist's Conk. Rusty-colored spores have covered everything under the mushroom. CREDIT: ALEXIS MURRAY

There is a similarity between polypores and boletes. Both have, instead of gills or teeth, tubes or pores under their caps to produce spores. The easy difference between them is that the tubes on the underside of a bolete can be peeled away from the cap flesh without much trouble, but the pores under a polypore cap cannot be separated from the cap without damaging the cap. Beyond that, boletes are fleshy where as polypores tend to have a wood-like texture (with a few exceptions).

Most polypores are too tough to be considered food, but some of the fleshy ones are sought after.

Albatrellopsis confluens. The green bits on the caps are the start of a mold that is quite common on these. CREDIT: IKUKO LUBOW

FUSED POLYPORE
Albatrellopsis confluens

Family: Albatrellaceae

Ecology: Common in the Rockies, widely distributed, montane to subalpine ecosystems; fruiting late July through September. Mycorrhizal with conifers; spruce and fir.

Description: Cap medium to large, convex, often fused with the caps of others; cream color buff, pinkish buff, light orange-brown in age. Cracking dry surface with age. Often becoming moldy and green. The stem is short, of average thickness; central or a bit off center; white to buff in age, sometimes orange-brown at base. The underside of the cap is packed with almost undetectable tubes 2–5 millimeters deep, 3–5 pores/millimeter, pure white to straw yellow in age, running down the stem. The flesh is firm, breakable, white, cream to buff, staining tan. The spore print is white. The odor is pleasant, fragrant, or like Fruity Pebbles cereal.

Edibility: Edible when young. Mild, sometimes bitter tasting. Consuming large quantities could result in a laxative effect.

Look-alikes: *A. ovinus* is white and can be differentiated by a lighter colored and smoother cap.

Notes: Confluens, meaning running together and are often found growing in large masses, fused at the cap or base.

Greening Goat's Foot. There aren't many mushrooms with a cap this scaly. CREDIT: JOSEPH O'HALLARON

CROCODILE POLYPORE, GREENING GOAT'S FOOT
Albatrellus ellisii

Family: Albatrellaceae

Ecology: Found west of the Rockies, uncommon, montane to subalpine ecosystems; fruiting late July through September. Mycorrhizal with conifers; spruce and fir.

Description: Cap medium to large, convex to plane, wavy; hairy surface, forming scales with age; greenish to yellow-brown, often a mixture of colors. The stem is short, average to thick; off-center or lateral, solid; Greenish to yellow-brown, often a mixture of colors. The cap underside is packed with almost undetectable tiny tubes, white, staining green in age or when bruised, running down the stem. The flesh is firm, breakable, white, bruises green slowly. The spore print is white. The odor is mild.

Edibility: Edible. Has a pleasant chewy texture.

Look-alikes: *A. confluens,* when moldy.

Notes: Not a common fungus in the front range of the Rockies. Can be found west and north in British Columbia.

The pores are shallow, large, and run down the stem.

Albatrellus ovinus. Yellow colors just starting. CREDIT: ROY HALLING

SHEEP'S POLYPORE
Albatrellus ovinus

Family: Albatrellaceae

Ecology: Common in the Rockies, at higher elevations, fruiting late July through September. Mycorrhizal with conifers; spruce and fir.

Description: The cap is medium to large, convex and irregular, whitish buff to cream colored, yellowing in the cracking surface. Sometimes fused with other caps. The stem is short and of average thickness; central or eccentric; cream colored to pinkish to pinkish brown. The underside of the cap is packed with fine tubes, sometimes running down the stem. The flesh is firm, breakable, cream to buff. The spore print is white. The odor is pleasant, aromatic.

Edibility: Edible when young and cooked well. Mild tasting. Consuming large quantities could result in a laxative effect.

Look-alikes: *A. confluens* can be differentiated by cinnamon cream or pinkish colored caps that sometimes appear cracked or scaly.

Notes: This mushroom fruit is fleshy and firm. I find it growing on the north x east steeper slopes, where it's cooler and wetter. It grows solitary to scattered or gregarious.

Artist's Conk. Note the dusting of rusty brown spores.

ARTIST'S CONK
Ganoderma applanatum

Family: Polyporaceae

Ecology: Saprophyte, growing in aspen forests all through the Rockies, year-round; sometimes on dead or decaying hardwoods.

Description: The mushroom is large, fan-shaped, and the upper surface is dry, tough, furrowed and wavy; the underside is white to light brown tubes in layers that bruise easily and oxidize to brown very quickly. The flesh is light brown when young and darkens to red-brown later, appearing rusty or faded on the top from the spores. The spores are rusty brown and often cover the mushroom and everything nearby.

Edibility: Very tough and woodlike. Not exactly edible, but it is sometimes dried and powdered and used then to make tea or tinctures.

Look-alikes: *Fomitopsis pinicola* group but easily differentiated by the bruising of the hymenium.

Notes: The artist's conk is a larger, shelf-like mushroom and the only *Ganoderma* sp. that grows in Colorado. Related to the famous *G. lucidum,* this prolific spore producer is famous for the canvas provided on the underside of the cap. Using pressure, generations of humans have sketched beautiful images on the underside of the artist's conk. Oxidation soon reveals a brown tracing of the artist's movements.

Turkey Tails. A very close look at the cap will reveal that the zones alternate between being fuzzy and smooth.

TURKEY TAIL
Trametes versicolor

Family: Hymenochaetaceae

Ecology: Saprophytic, growing on dead or decaying hardwoods all over the state. Common July through September.

Description: The caps are small to medium, semi-circular, often growing in rosette clusters, velvety or hairy, sometimes leathery, with colorful zones or rings featuring an array of colors: brown, red-brown, green, blue-gray, gray, buff, pale yellow. There is no stem. The underside of the cap has super small, difficult to perceive tubes that are white to buff. The flesh is tough and pliable. The spore print is white.

Edibility: Inedible; its very tough. Can be decocted into a nice tea with lemon and honey or extracted for tincture using alcohol and water (dual extraction).

Look-alikes: Stereum species are often confused for turkey tail. Easily differentiated by examining the underside. Stereum lacks pores.

Notes: A very common mushroom growing across the globe. Has been studied in Japan for its immunomodulating effects and its promise as a powerful ally with cancer treatments.

RECIPE

Turkey Tail Tea

BY ED LUBOW

Ingredients

2 to 4 grams of dried turkey tails cut into small pieces or powdered

1 cup boiling water

Optional Ingredients

Sweetener (sugar, honey, etc.)

Milk, half-and-half, cream

Spices (ginger, cardamom, etc.)

Other flavorings (tea, cocoa, etc.)

Preparation

1. Steep as you would most teas, about 3 minutes.

2. Enjoy

While this recipe specifies turkey tails, most dried mushrooms could be used. The optional ingredients you use will depend on your tastes and the taste of the mushrooms used.

6. Tooth Fungi

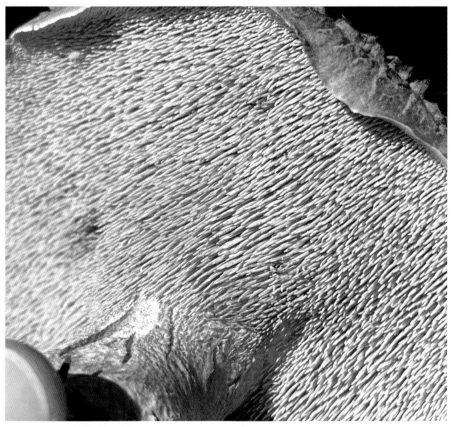

The teeth are actually soft and fleshy to the touch. CREDIT: ALEX MERRYMAN

by Orion Aon

We call the mushrooms in this group toothed because of their spore-bearing structures. Instead of gills, these mushrooms have sharp, narrow teeth or stalactite-like structures that hang down and release spores at maturity. Toothed mushrooms come in many forms, from small mycorrhizal species to large saprotrophic and parasitic species. They are some of the safest wild mushrooms because they have no toxic species and are often easy to identify. Though many species in this group are too woody or bitter-tasting to be edible, a handful are delicacies. The species below are not genetically close, but all have teeth and are delicious.

In addition to the edible species listed below, there are several species of tooth mushrooms with non-culinary uses. One example is the intensely vanilla-smelling *Hydnellum suaveolens*. This mushroom looks relatively plain from the top but has a vibrant violet stem underground and, when dried, can be used as a natural blue dye.

Sarcodon imbricatus. Slightly dented in the center and adorned with large dark scales. Very firm consistency. CREDIT: ORION AON

HAWK'S WING OR SHINGLED HEDGEHOG
Sarcodon imbricatus

Family: Bankeraceae

Ecology: Found growing in clusters or strings above about 8,000 feet in July and August. They are mycorrhizal with spruce (*Picea* spp.) and fir (*Abies* spp.) trees and prefer habitats with extra moisture, such as mountain streams or north-facing slopes.

Description: Tan to brown caps with dark, raised scales resembling a hawk's wing pattern. Their stems are short, central, and can become hollow. Their spore print is light brown to brown. These mushrooms often have fly larvae in the stems and are occasionally eaten by wildlife.

Edibility: Edible but can become tough and bitter at maturity. Some people find these quite bitter or metallic tasting at all stages of growth. Note that there is at least one look-alike species that is extremely bitter and inedible. If you taste your specimens (a lick of a broken piece off the cap) you will be able to easily avoid the bitter ones.

Note the delicate white teeth and the slight staining on the stalk. CREDIT: ROY HALLING

HEDGEHOG OR SWEET TOOTH
Hydnum spp.

Family: Hydnaceae

Ecology: They grow above 8,000 feet in elevation under spruce (*Picea* spp.) and fir (*Abies* spp.) trees and prefer habitats with more moisture such as mountain streams or north-facing slopes.

Description: They are small and fragile, with peach-colored caps and delicate teeth. For some, the stalk is mostly white but can have some pale peach–colored tints or staining. These mushrooms are relatively rare in the Southern Rocky Mountains but are a delight to find and a choice edible species. They are similar in flavor and texture to chanterelles.

Edibility: Choice edible.

Hericium coralloides. Note the hanging teeth at the ends of the branching cluster. CREDIT: JOSEPH O'HALLARON

CORAL TOOTH, LION'S MANE
Hericium coralloides

Family: Hericiaceae

Ecology: These mushrooms are rare to find in the Southern Rocky Mountains. Here, they tend to fruit from cottonwood logs in the mid-elevation riparian areas from late summer into fall.

Description: They grow in a cluster of branches reaching from a central core, each branch decorated with delicate hanging teeth. They start white but become tinted yellow and eventually brown as they mature. Their spore color is white.

Edibility: Choice edible.

RECIPE

Pickled Hawk's Wing Escabeche

BY JAMES CHELIN

Yield: About 4 to 6 one-ounce mason jars

Ingredients:
4 cups hawk's wing mushrooms sliced ¼ inch thick
4 medium carrots peeled and cut into ½-inch-thick slices
1 medium sweet onion cut into 1-inch pieces
6 jalapeños and/or serranos (hotter) sliced lengthwise
2 to 3 tablespoons olive oil
1 tablespoon sea salt + more to taste
1 tablespoon sugar
1 tablespoon peppercorns
4 garlic cloves crushed
1 teaspoon Mexican oregano
2 bay leaves
2 cups apple cider vinegar
4 cups water
Additional water for bath if canning

Preparation:
1. Clean your hawk's wings with a brush to remove any spruce needles or dirt.
2. Heat a large pot on medium high heat; then add the olive oil, onions, hawk's wings, carrots, chilies, and garlic.
3. Cook for about 5–10 minutes stirring often until the onions start turning translucent.
4. Add the salt and stir.
5. Add the water, vinegar, bay leaves, sugar, oregano, and peppercorns and bring to a boil.
6. Taste the mixture with a spoon. Add additional salt and vinegar to taste if necessary.
7. Cook for about 10 minutes.

Note: If you like to spice things up, use only serranos instead of jalapeños.

If you're not canning, you can let the mixture cool and store in the refrigerator for up to 2 weeks. Let cool overnight before eating.

For Canning
1. Ladle into sterilized jars and put the lids on.
2. Using a canning pot, place the jars in a boiling hot water bath for 10 minutes.
3. Remove the jars and let cool.
4. Label the jars and write the date on the labels with a Sharpie.

They can be stored on the shelf at room temperature for up to 2 years. Once you open a jar, it should then be stored in the refrigerator. They taste best after 2 weeks of pickling time. Serve as a side dish with your favorite Mexican food.

Pickled Hawk's Wing Escabeche. CREDIT: JAMES CHELIN

7. Jelly Fungi

Tree ears are the largest jelly fungi you are likely to find. CREDIT: JACOB RONDER

by Natalie Hyde and Patricia Bukur

As the name suggests, jelly fungi have a gelatinous texture, although a better description might be that they are mostly fairly tough and rubbery. Most are small and won't be noticed unless you are looking for them.

Tree Ears. These are most common on fallen subalpine fir trees in late summer. CREDIT: GINGER McKEY

WOOD EAR, JELLY EAR
Auricularia americana

Family: Auriculariacea

Ecology: Appears in early summer to late fall in montane and subalpine ecosystems. Saprobic on decaying conifer logs or sticks. Often occurring on subalpine fir logs in Colorado.

Description: Fruiting body forms gelatinous, irregular ear-like shallow cups. Flesh is thin, rubbery, and brown to reddish brown with fine hairs on the surface. When young its underside can appear frosted with a whitish dusting, but this disappears once developed. Matures to 2–10 centimeters across and is directly attached to wood without a stalk. Can be confused with a few ascomycete cup fungi based on similar shapes such as *Peziza*, but these cup fungi are brittle and grow on the ground. Odor and taste are mild.

Edibility: Edible, but no flavor. Widely used in eastern Asia for medicinal purposes and cuisine such as Hot and Sour soup, where it adds a surprisingly crunchy texture.

The upper surface of tree ears are often interestingly ribbed. CREDIT: PATRICIA BUKUR

Witch's Butter. Most common on dead aspen and never on conifer wood. CREDIT: RON WOLF

WITCH'S BUTTER
Tremella mesenterica

Family: Tremellaceae

Ecology: Appears in early summer through October in subalpine and mixed hardwood forests. Commonly found growing alone or in amorphous clusters on sticks and logs of decaying deciduous trees. *Tremella* species are obligate mycoparasites. *T. mesenterica* is a parasite of the genus *Peniophora* (a crust fungus found growing on hardwood bark). *Peniophora* may not be present to the visible eye as *T. mesenterica* can parasitize the mycelium of *Peniophora* without the presence of a fruiting body.

Description: Lobes appear in brain-like clusters about 2–5 centimeters across and 1–3 centimeters high. Flesh is dull to bright yellow or orangish yellow gelatinous to rubbery with a smooth and moist surface. The fruiting body will wither and shrink in dry

Orange Jelly. These are very similar to witch's butter but grow on dead conifer wood. CREDIT: IAN FIERMAN

conditions, becoming hard and turning a darker pigment, then revive when moisture returns. It is commonly confused with *Dacrymyces chrysospermus*. However *D. chrysospermus* has a whitish attachment point to its substrate, is typically smaller in size, and grows on conifers. Odor and taste are nondistinctive.

Edibility: Nonpoisonous. The gelatinous to rubbery consistency leads some to suggest it as inedible, but it is commonly used in medicinal soup recipes in China.

RECIPE

Chinese Hot and Sour Soup

BY IKUKO LUBOW

Rehydrate

½ cup dried shiitake mushrooms (or 2 cups fresh)

¼ cup dried wood ear mushrooms

¼ cup dried lily flowers

Marinade

½ pound (230 grams) pork loin cut into thin strips

½ tablespoon grated ginger in rice wine

½ tablespoon soy sauce

½ tablespoon corn starch

½ teaspoon sesame oil

Soup

¼ cup vegetable oil

1 small can of bamboo shoots, rinsed

¼ cup Chinese red vinegar

6 cups water or chicken stock

1 block tofu

½ cup soy sauce

3 tablespoons water chestnut starch mixed with 2 tablespoons water

2 eggs beaten

1 teaspoon sesame oil

2 tablespoons crushed red pepper

Preparation

For those who are vegetarian, pork strips are optional.

1. Mix marinade ingredients and let it sit for 20 minutes.
2. When shiitake, wood ear, and lily flowers are rehydrated, drain liquid.
3. Add vegetable oil in a pot and stir-fry the bamboo shoots and rehydrated materials.
4. Add soy sauce, Chinese red vinegar, and 6 cups of water/chicken stock (I prefer chicken stock) and bring to a boil.
5. Drain most of the marinade liquid and add the pork and tofu to the pot along with the crushed hot pepper. Turn down the heat to medium and continue cooking until pork is cooked completely.
6. At this point, adjust the overall flavor of the soup. Remember that it's supposed to be hot and sour as the primary flavors. Add hot pepper and vinegar as appropriate to taste.
7. Add 2 tablespoons of water to the eggs and beat them thoroughly.
8. Slowly add the eggs to the pot, making a circular motion while pouring it in, and do not stir.
9. Gently pour water chestnut mixture into the pot.

Enjoy!

8. Coral Fungi

Typical yellow coral mushrooms. CREDIT: GINGER McKEY

by James Chelin and Jennifer Bell

This is a mysterious group—interesting, beautiful, and occasionally edible if not choice.

They often look like their namesake in the ocean and it's odd to see them branching out, scattered on a hillside at 9,000 feet!

Colors vary from white to yellow, orange, tan, pink, and purple.

Clavariadelphus truncatus, or club coral, is the best of this group to cook and eat. The late famed mycologist Gary Lincoff liked to cook meals of many courses with mushrooms featured in every dish, serving club coral for des-

sert. It has a strong sweetness and would taste right at home in a doughnut or ice cream. These are larger and grow in small groups on the ground.

Ramaria species resemble cauliflower especially when sliced open. They grow in small clumps.

Artomyces pyxidatus, or crown-tipped coral, is saprophytic and can be found growing from old wood and rotting stumps.

Coral mushrooms are also fine photo subjects.
CREDIT: RON WOLF

Ramarias also come in lovely pink. CREDIT: IAN FIERMAN

A bright yellow-orange Ramaria. CREDIT: GINGER McKEY

YELLOW RAMARIA
Ramaria spp.

Family: Gomphaceae

Ecology: Grows on the ground at higher elevations usually under spruce or other conifers. Very often growing in large arcs or rings pushing up through the soil. They are found mostly in the summer through early fall.

Description: The fruiting body consists of medium to large clumps, with numerous branches, forming rounded a treelike structure with a thick stalk. When sliced open, they are very reminiscent of cauliflower. The flesh is yellow to orange. Solid white firm flesh on the inside when cut or pulled apart. Aging to a light brown on the edges especially the tips. The smell is mushroomy. A spore print will be yellow.

Edibility: Edible with caution.

A large yellow Ramaria. CREDIT: JAMES CHELIN

Look-alikes: In our area there are many similar Ramaria species that are difficult to identify by macroscopic features alone. It is best to avoid any that are peppery, bitter, or blueish green staining as some of those species could be poisonous. Stick to yellowish orange varieties before they get too old, turn too brown, or become gelatinous. Less common are members of the genus *Lentaria*, which can be distinguished by being much less brittle than Ramarias.

Notes: Some people may have adverse reactions or laxative effects from consuming Ramaria species. It's best to sample a small portion at first and avoid eating large quantities. In moderation they are fine for most people. They actually make a pretty good trail jerky. It is common to find them filled with dirt and old spruce needles. When peeling them apart a small brush is really helpful for cleaning them. *Ramaria largentii* is a common orange variety in the Rocky Mountains.

Crown-Tipped Coral. This is an unusually large specimen. CREDIT: MAIA REED

CROWN-TIPPED CORAL
Artomyces pyxidatus

Family: Auriscalpiaceae

Ecology: Growing on dead deciduous logs and stumps. Usually found on aspen in our area. Growing early summer to early fall.

Description: White to a pale yellow with a crown-shaped tip aging to brown. Thin, rounded and branching from a common base. The flesh is pale yellowish white, fairly fragile, turning brown with age. The odor is mild and the spore print is white.

Edibility: Edible.

Notes: Often found in small groups growing on dead wood. One of the only corals that grows directly on rotting logs and stumps. It is thinner with more branching than Ramaria species. Sometimes they can be prolific but usually it can be difficult to find enough to make a meal.

Truncated Club. These are actually sugary sweet. CREDIT: JAMES CHELIN

CLUB CORAL, TRUNCATED CLUB
Clavariadelphus truncatus

Family:
Ecology: Scattered in small groups on the ground in needle duff under conifers. Occurring summer through early fall.
Description: The fruiting body is club shaped with rounded edges, wrinkled, sometimes cracking at the tip with age. They are larger and more robust than other coral mushrooms. The flesh inside is white and fibrous. The odor is mild, and the taste sweet. The spore print is white to pale yellow.
Edibility: Edible.
Notes: We have more than one variety in the Rocky Mountains. *C. truncatus var truncatus* is larger, more robust, and has yellowish spores and a flat club-shaped cap. *C. truncatus var lovejoyae* has a more rounded cap, white spores, and reddish colors. *C. ligula* is a closely related mushroom that is yellow and much smaller. It grows on the ground gregariously in "troops" usually by the hundreds. It is also edible but usually not worth collecting due to its small size.

RECIPE

Ramaria Jerky

BY JAMES CHELIN

Ingredients

About 4 cups Ramaria coral mushrooms

1 cup organic soy sauce

¼ cup water

1 tablespoon honey

2 tablespoons lemon juice

1 teaspoon garlic powder

1 teaspoon minced ginger

1 teaspoon red pepper flakes (optional; spicy)

Preparation

1. Clean your coral mushrooms by removing any dirt or forest debris.
2. Separate them by hand into ¼-inch strips and put into a large bowl.
3. In a separate bowl mix together the lemon juice and honey first. Next mix in the soy sauce, water, and spices.
4. Mix the marinade mixture gently with the mushrooms being careful not to break them.
5. Marinate in the refrigerator for several hours or overnight (stronger flavor).
6. Drain the marinade and place mushrooms evenly on a dehydrator set to 135–160° F.
7. Dehydrate for several hours up to ½ day until all mushrooms are dried.

Note: Dehydrating longer or at higher temperatures will make them very crispy. If you like your jerky less crispy, use a lower temperature and monitor periodically to remove when fairly dry but still pliable.

Ramaria Jerky.
CREDIT: JAMES CHELIN

9. Ink Caps

Mica Caps. These come up all over town after some good rains. CREDIT: ALEXIS MURRAY

by Ginger McKey

This is a large group of mushrooms united by having gills that are not attached to the stem, a black or very dark spore print color, and that they break down into an ink-like slime as they age. Most are small, and only a couple are worth trying to eat.

Shaggy Mane. These often come up in parks. CREDIT: JOSEPH O'HALLARON

Shaggy Mane, *Coprinus comatus*. Some are starting to get inky and decomposing near the edges. Younger ones are best. CREDIT: IAN FIERMAN

SHAGGY MANE
Coprinus comatus

Family: Agaricaceae

Ecology: Appearing June to October, alone or in clusters, in nutrient-rich soil in meadows, lawns, gardens, and roadside and riparian areas, from low to high elevation.

Description: Caps are medium in size, oval in shape, and close to the stalk when young, then become bell-shaped and curling upward at the edges as they mature. Young caps are mostly white, with a light brown tint at the top and fine white scales covering the surface. As the caps mature, the scales darken and become more pronounced, giving the surface a shaggy appearance. Flesh is white, thin, and fragile. The gills of young specimens are white, becoming pink and then inky black and liquefying, from the lower edges inward. Stalk is smooth, white, brittle, and straight, sometimes with a small movable ring near the base. Odor and taste are mild.

Edibility: Edible and excellent. Choose caps that are young with pale gills. They should be cooked very soon after collecting, as they can begin to degrade quickly.

Mica Cap, *Coprinellus micaceus*. Often clustered; pale brown color with the mica-like scales. Best before it gets inky at the edges when mature. CREDIT: RON WOLF

MICA CAP
Coprinellus micaceus

Family: Psathyrellaceae

Ecology: Appearing April to October, in dense clusters on rotting wood, wood debris, or over buried decaying wood along roadsides, open grassy areas, and beneath old trees, often in urban settings.

Description: Caps are small in size, oval in shape when young, and become bell-shaped and often split along the edges as they mature. They are pale buff, honey brown or cinnamon brown in color, with striations extending inward. Caps are covered with fine, mica-like granules that may wash off with dew or rain. Flesh is pale brown and thin. Gills are pale buff when young, darkening to black with age. Stalk is white, fibrous, hollow, and brittle without a ring. Odor and taste are mild to not distinctive.

Edibility: Edible, but not noteworthy.

RECIPE

Cream of Shaggy Mane Soup

BY ED LUBOW (ADAPTED FROM A RECIPE BY HOPE MILLER)

Ingredients

1 quart fresh shaggy manes cut into bite-sized pieces
1 tablespoon butter (for sauteing mushrooms)
½ cup butter (for soup base)
½ cup flour
2 quarts whole milk
Salt and pepper to taste

Optional Ingredients

¼ teaspoon ground nutmeg
Pinch of dried, powdered hot pepper such as cayenne
Dry sherry
Cognac

Preparation

1. Saute the mushrooms in 1 tablespoon of butter. Reserve the liquid.
2. Melt ½ cup of butter in a large saucepan; then add the flour, stirring to avoid lumps until thickened.
3. Add milk and stir until it thickens.
4. Add the rest of the ingredients and the reserved liquid from the first step.

This is basically a good general cream of mushroom soup recipe that can be adapted for most mushrooms.

10. Russula and Lactarius

Typical Shrimp Russulas. CREDIT: RON WOLF

by Ian Fierman

The genus *Russula* composes a very large group of mushrooms within the family Russulaceae, containing at least 750 known species worldwide and close to half of them are found in North America. They are commonly known as "brittle-gills" due to their general nature of being quite frail and crumbly, with only a few exceptions, like some in section *Compactae*. These mushrooms are quite common during summer months in the mountains, often spanning a relatively long growing season. Caps range from small to large (3–30 centimeters across) and many *Russula* mushrooms are brightly colored, making them hard to miss.

In this chapter we will cover the species found in our area of the Southern Rockies with a focus on those which are considered some of the easiest to identify and also have no toxic look-alikes, so there is very little possibility of confusion.

Red Russula. This russula is hot peppery (acrid) and should not be eaten. CREDIT: RON WOLF

To identify mushrooms in the genus *Russula* using macromorphology (naked eye without a microscope), here are a few tricks:

- The spore color of these mushrooms can range from an almost pure white or yellowish to a burnt orange, ocher, or amber color, so taking a spore print can often come in handy when narrowing things down to species.
- Take a little nibble of the mushroom, chew at the tip of your tongue, and keep that going for 15–20 seconds, then spit it out. If there is any sort of taste or sensation other than that of raw mushroom, such as a tingling feeling, or a bitter, acrid, or spicy flavor, then the mushroom is usually considered inedible. This approach is only to be used in conjunction with other methods of ID mentioned because there is always the chance that the sensation or flavor is less present or the taste-tester misses it, but it is a completely safe scientific technique used for this genus and other mushrooms in the Russulaceae family.
- Finally, peel the skin on the cap back and see how far it goes before detaching. This may sound odd but when you have done it with a few different species it starts to make sense, as some will peel all of the way to the center of the cap, while others can barely be peeled back before tearing away from the cap, and this can be a discerning factor for identification.

Never consume red-capped Russula mushrooms with acrid, bitter, or spicy flavors.

Shrimp Russula. One of the most common and popular Russula species. CREDIT: RON WOLF

SHRIMP RUSSULA, CRAB BRITTLEGILL
Russula xerampelina group

Family: Russulaceae

Ecology: Common in midsummer through fall in soil under conifers in montane to sub-alpine habitats in the Southern Rockies. Scattered to gregarious or sometimes found in large groups.

Description: The medium-sized cap is irregularly round as a button, becoming flatter or sometimes with wavy edges. The colors are quite variable, from pale to dark blood-red, burgundy, or brown, sometimes with hints of pink, yellow, orange, gold, bronze, or green, frequently a mix of colors and sometimes only one, but usually with a darker center that has a slight dip in the middle. The cap can feel smooth or velvety and is sticky when wet. The skin peels around one-fourth of the cap's edge. Its gills are attached to the stem and off-white, becoming yellowish with brown stains.

The stem is medium-sized, sometimes with grooves running vertically. It is whitish, but usually with a rosy-red flush and turns brownish with age. If you scratch the surface of the stem it turns slightly yellow. The flesh stains green with the application of ferrous sulfate ($FeSO_4$). The "shrimp Russula" is mild tasting or sometimes pleasant and the odor is often mild in younger specimens, but it always develops a telltale seafood smell, usually soon after being picked but particularly if it is old, crushed, or contained in a paper bag for a bit. The spores are dark yellow to deep ocher in print.

Edibility: Choice! The flavor and texture of the cooked mushroom is like that of a slightly sweet meat.

Notes: This is one of the more sought after edibles and the easiest to identify of the reddish-capped Russula species. The shrimp Russula stores well if cooked and then frozen, and it is excellent when dried and powdered to be used as a thickener and flavor enhancer in dishes.

Although evidence points to this being at least a handful of very similar species lumped together under one name, the aroma of seafood is always present to varying degrees; they all stain green when ferrous sulfate is applied; they have yellow to ocher spore prints, brownish-staining flesh, and usually a pinkish-red tinge to the stem that when scratched will turn yellowish, altogether making these mushrooms quite distinct. Their coloration is very diverse and this could be due to the reason mentioned above regarding the likelihood that this is actually several closely related species forming a group.

Collectors should be wary of other red Russula mushrooms that do not exhibit these features as there are various reports of gastrointestinal poisonings in the region.

Graying Russula. Although common and easy to identify, not very good to eat. CREDIT: IKUKO LUBOW

COPPER BRITTLEGILL, GRAYING RUSSULA
Russula decolorans group

Family: Russulaceae

Ecology: Found in late summer and fall. Very common in much of the Southern Rocky Mountain region under lodgepole pine and other conifers in montane to subalpine habitats.

Description: The cap can be quite large and is bronze, orange, copper, or brick red, fading to a dull yellow or pale rose and eventually grayish ocher. It is rounded at first and becomes dish or vase shaped in maturity. The texture is smooth when dry and sticky when wet and the skin peels only at the margin. Its crowded gills are occasionally forked and they attach to the stem or run down it slightly. The gills are white or light yellow, discoloring gray when bruised or fading to gray when dry and/or old. The stem is often long, firm, and usually thicker at the base. It stains gray when bruised or with age, particularly the interior flesh. The taste is mild or occasionally alluding to a slight peppery quality in young gills. The spore print is cream-yellow to pale ocher.

Edibility: Sometimes palatable, never great. The larger the mushroom the worse the flavor and mealier the texture, so buttons are ideal.

Notes: Considered a complex of mushrooms which are altogether identical to the naked eye, this is one of the most abundant of the Russula species in the southern Rockies. At times they are the most common mushroom in an area, particularly on slopes with lodge-pole pines during dry spells in late summer. At first, the cap can be a pretty copper or bronze, but they always fade to a dirty grayish yellow when old and large. There are other yellowish species which are less common that occur in our area, but they are smaller, brighter in color, and mostly grow in wetter habitats than the pine duff–loving "copper brittlegill."

Short-Stemmed Russula. Probably best for hosting the lobster mushroom parasite.

SHORT-STEMMED RUSSULA, STUBBY BRITTLEGILL
Russula brevipes

Family: Russulaceae

Ecology: Relatively common in montane ecosystems from July to September. Grows alone or scattered in small groups of two or three under conifers, particularly lodgepole pine.

Despcription: The cap of this medium to large white mushroom is unevenly rounded at first, becoming vase shaped with age. They feel dry and felty and the skin does not peel easily from the cap's marginal edge. Gills are creamy to clay colored with a bluish green tint and they stain brown with age. The stem is short, stout, smooth, and dry and it is white but often stains brownish.

Edibility: Considered edible, but it often smells foul and it can have an overpowering peppery flavor.

Notes: Often encountered during the dry late summer months as "shrumps" (lumps) in the duff of lodgepole pine and other conifers. The *R. brevipes* that was initially described (Peck, New York, 1890) is edible and reportedly can be quite good. Collections here have often been referred to using the now obsolete name Russula brevipes var. acrior, and as the epithet suggests (*acrior* being "acrid"), our local "stubby brittlegill" is sharply peppery and somewhat unpleasant tasting in fresh specimens. *Lactarius deceptivus* resembles this species and often grows close by, but all mushrooms in the genus *Lactarius* exude a milky latex from the injured gills. Other Russula species with sometimes whitish caps are *R. albonigra* and *R. nigricans*, but their hard flesh turns black with age or when injured.

This mushroom is a host to *Hypomyces lactifluorum*, which is the parasitic fungus responsible for forming lobster mushrooms. The infection takes over the Russula, eventually changing its outward appearance entirely from a gilled white mushroom into a sort of warped orange mass, somewhat resembling a large and malformed chanterelle mushroom. It is considered a highly prized edible and is sought after in places like the Midwest and both coasts of North America, where they are much more commonly encountered than here. In the Southern Rocky Mountain region they are evasive and less numerous but always a joy for the fungal forager to find.

Green Russula. One of the few grass green-capped Russulas.

GRASS-GREEN RUSSULA, TACKY GREEN RUSSULA
Russula aeruginea

Family: Russulaceae

Ecology: Summer and fall. Growing alone, scattered, or dispersed in small groups in mixed woods under aspen from montane to subalpine zones. Common and often abundant in the Southern Rockies.

Description: The cap is small and cushion-shaped at first, becoming flat or slightly depressed as the mushroom matures. Grayish olive green to yellowish-green in color, sometimes with brown or yellow blotches and usually with a darker green center. It is smooth and shiny, never cracked, and is tacky when young, slippery when wet. The margin is often thin and furrowed and peels halfway. Its brittle gills are crowded and sometimes forked near the stem. They are whitish to creamy yellow, usually with brown stains, particularly in older specimens. The stem is small, short, and cylindrical or with a tapered base. It is white or faintly yellowish and often has rust-brown stains present at the base. *R. aeruginea* has flesh that is white and brittle. The taste and smell are indistinct or mildly fungal. Spores are cream to pale yellow or pale ocher.

Edibility: Edible and decent. Mild in flavor, so it does well on its own or incorporated into mixed-mushroom dishes. Generally speaking, the buttons of Russula are usually preferred for the dinner table and this one isn't an exception, so go for the smaller ones.

Notes: In the Southern Rockies, *R. aeruginea* seems to have a fondness for aspen trees and is often found growing in grass, sometimes in or especially around the edge of an aspen grove. There are a few Russula in the region that are green or can be from time to time, which may superficially resemble *R. aeruginea* from a distance, but the smooth yellow-green cap that is tacky, particularly when young; the gills and base of stem which both frequently stain brownish; and the yellowish spore print altogether make this an easily recognized species.

Other green Russulas: If you have identified a mushroom to the genus, green Russula species are always a safe bet for the forager.

Russula parvovirescens aka the blue-green cracked Russula, or quilted green Russula, can be found growing alone or widely dispersed in mixed woods of montane to subalpine ecosystems from summer into the early fall months. The cap of *R. parvovirescens* is round, firm, and grayish green at first, eventually turning more of a bluish sea-green and flattening out on top with a silken-feeling surface, and it is made up of dry, cracked, chalky little patches. It is edible. Nice and crunchy in younger specimens! This mushroom was formerly called *R. viriscens* but that name is now used for a different European species and can possibly be applied to some eastern forms in the United States as well. Our western *R. parvovirescens* is generally more blue in color and is now considered a genetically distinct species. This particular coloration along with the cracked cap and white spore print are good diagnostic characteristics for field identification. *R. aeruginea* has a cap that is tacky and smooth, greenish but never blue-green, and the spore color is yellowish.

Russula olivacea is another mushroom that can appear in a range of colors but usually includes a greenish olive in the cap, as the name *olivacea* suggests. These mushrooms are encountered from midsummer through fall, sometimes found growing alone but more often in troops. In Europe they are found with hardwoods like beech, but in our region they prefer mixed woods with spruce in montane to subalpine forests. *R. olivacea* has a large cap that is yellowish when young, then burgundy to olive green or some mix of colors. The gills are a pale yellow or dull ochre and usually reddish near the margin and the spore print is yellow to deep ochre-orange in print. Its stem is medium to large, firm and white with a rose-pink flush toward the top near the gills (apex). The olive brittlegill tastes mild and doesn't smell like much in the field. It is an excellent edible and is similar to the shrimp Russula in its somewhat sweet and meaty flavor. The occasionally colossal cap size, often with some mixture of greens, reds, purples and yellows, along with the flush of pink on the stem, are helpful features for identification.

RECIPE

Shrimp Russula Risotto*

BY MICHAEL B. HEIM

Serves: 4 people

Ingredients

12 ounces *Russula xerampelina* (shrimp Russula) mushrooms—cleaned, brushed, tamped dry, sliced thin
1 small onion (shallot) finely chopped
2 tablespoons extra virgin olive oil
2 tablespoons unsalted butter
12 ounces Arborio or Carnaroli rice
3 pints mushroom stock** or chicken stock
Salt and fresh pepper to taste
Nob of butter
Parmesan cheese
Dill or thyme
Lemon (optional)

Preparation

1. Saute onion in the oil and butter until it colors, add the mushrooms, and continue to fry over medium+ heat for 2 minutes. If using dried mushrooms add to the mix now.
2. Add the rice and continuously stir using a wooden spoon for about 2 minutes or until the rice is coated in the oil and butter.
3. Add the stock or reserved liquid one ladle at a time. Preferably the stock is already simmering. As the rice absorbs the liquid, while continuously stirring, add more liquid. Do this for about 20 minutes.
4. Once al dente, remove from heat, season, and finish with the nob of butter and freshly grated parmesan.
5. Add fresh herbs like dill or thyme to finish. A squeeze of lemon will brighten this nicely.

* Adapted Anotonio Carluccio recipe.
** If you would like to enhance flavor, use homemade mushroom stock or dried shrimp Russula. Simply reconstitute the dried mushrooms in a small bowl of filtered water or stock for 15 minutes. Reserve liquid for risotto stock later.

RECIPE

Lactarius Mushrooms on Toast

BY MICHAEL B. HEIM

Yields 1 plate

Ingredients

1.5 cups Lactarius mushrooms—cleaned, brushed, tamped dry, sliced lengthwise

1 tablespoon, freshly chopped thyme, tarragon, chives, parsley

2 tablespoons butter, extra virgin olive oil, or pancetta + fat

3 tablespoons heavy cream or goat cheese

Sherry vinegar or fresh squeeze of lemon

Salt and pepper to taste

Preparation

1. Saute Lactarius in butter, cooking off the water and allowing the mushrooms to achieve some color. **Wait to salt.** Then add the cream or goat cheese and reduce until it has coated the mushrooms. Add thyme, tarragon, chives, parsley, salt, and pepper.

2. Finish with sherry vinegar or a lemon squeeze and serve over grilled baguette, scrambled eggs, or fresh pasta.

11. Agaricus and Similar

Agaricus. The gills have become the characteristic dark chocolate brown color of the ripe spores.
CREDIT: MAIA REED

by James Chelin and Jennifer Bell

If there is a picture in a dictionary of a mushroom, it is probably an Agaricus.

When people buy mushrooms at the market, they are most commonly *Agaricus bisporus*. They were given names by marketers: white button, cremini, and portobello—all the same fungus at various stages of development.

Wild Agaricus species, on the other hand, are difficult to discern—each from the other. They look a lot alike.

They have more than appearance in common. They are all saprobes eating up dead organic matter such as pine needles and fallen pieces of bark. They always grow on the ground.

With a few exceptions they are edible if not choice. Be cautious of yellow-staining Agaricus as some can be mildly poisonous.

Shaggy Parasols. They don't look like Agaricus, but they are fairly closely related. CREDIT: IKUKO LUBOW

The Friendly Agaricus. The red-staining dark-capped Agaricus under spruce at high altitudes. CREDIT: JAMES CHELIN

FRIENDLY AGARICUS
Agaricus amicosus
by James Chelin

Family: Agaricaceae

Ecology: You can look for it at higher elevations under Engelmann spruce growing straight up through the bark and needle duff on the ground. Typically growing in small groups of usually three or more. Grows from July through September.

Description: A rather large, robust woodland Agaricus that stains a reddish orange (rather than yellow) where nicked or scratched. It has a light brown reddish cap that is fibrous, scaly with cottony fibrils, and a mottled pattern turning darker with age. Usually very thick and meaty. The gills are initially pink and turn brown at maturity, not attached to the stem. They turn darker where injured or scratched from sticks as they push up through the conifer debris. The stem is initially white with a grainy pattern going down the stem, turning a lighter brown with age starting at the top going all the way down with a thinner skirted sheathlike ring that can be cottony on the underside. The flesh is initially white, staining a reddish orange color especially when sliced. The smell is mushroomy and the spore print is dark chocolate brown.

Edibility: Edible.

Notes: *A. amicosus* is always a delight to find and is a great portobello substitute. When cooked they darken much more in color compared to other Agaricus. They're great paired with a steak and a glass of red wine. They also work well as a meat substitute in tacos, mushroom burgers, and other dishes. Could be confused with *Agaricus julius*, which grows in similar habitats and is also a fantastic edible.

The Horse Mushroom. The details on the underside of the ring are important for identification.
CREDIT: RON WOLF

THE HORSE MUSHROOM
Agaricus arvensis
by James Chelin, Jennifer Bell

Family: Agaricaceae

Ecology: This is a fungus that loves the same valleys and grassy meadows that horses do—hence, the common name. It also thrives on suburban lawns. Because it is so good to eat, you must think twice about the fertilizers or weed killers you may also be ingesting. Look for *A. arvensis* along the front range late spring to early summer. Sometimes they reappear in the early fall.

Description: The cap is medium to large in size, round and hemispheric in appearance. It is quite white at first, yellowing slightly where injured on the cap. It darkens, becoming slightly brown in the center at maturity. The veil displays a classic cogwheel pattern when young. The gills appear white at first, then blushing to pink and eventually becoming chocolate brown at maturity. They are crowded and not attached to the stem. The stem is thick and round with a lovely skirt-like ring that turns yellowish below the ring at maturity. The meat of this mushroom is soft. You will notice yellowing that occurs during handling. The smell is delightful! Notes of cherry, almond, or anise. The spore print is dark chocolate brown.

Notes: Agaricus in Sect. Xanthodermatei are poisonous impostors, but the smell will tell you the difference. Also known as *Agaricus xanthodermus*; however, in our area we have a similar related mushroom from the same section of Agaricus called Xanthodermatei. Both fungi like the same habitat and both turn yellow when handled. However, Xanthodermatei types usually fruit a little later and generally have a long, curved stem that turns chrome yellow at the base when fresh. The stem is generally longer than the width of the cap at maturity, curved with a thick, felt-like ring. It smells unpleasant with a chemical odor similar to that of a chalkboard especially when a small piece is crushed. The smell of this mushroom is one of its key features. Unfortunately, not all people can smell the different odors of various Agaricus.

Salt-Loving Mushroom. The very firm texture and red staining make this common park resident distinctive. CREDIT: JAMES CHELIN

SALT-LOVING MUSHROOM
Agaricus bernardii
by James Chelin, Jennifer Bell

Family: Agaricaceae

Ecology: After the spring storms *A. bernardii* makes its appearance in suburban areas around the same time as daffodils. This Agaricus pops up in disturbed areas, also in irrigated lawns and especially where salt is used to clear the roads of ice—hence the common name.

Description: Husky, beefy, and short with some of the largest specimens to be found in the state of Colorado. The cap has a fairly distinct in-rolled margin. The top of the cap sometimes cracks and you'll see it darkening somewhat at maturity. The gills are initially a delightful pink color, browning as it ages. Gills are crowded and not attached to the stem. The stem is thick and of average height. The flesh is thick and shows intense reddening when the fungus is cut or injured. The smell is briny, like the ocean, and the spore print is dark chocolate brown.

Edibility: Yes.

Notes: This fungus stands out from other Agaricus because of its large size and thickness. They can be gregarious or grow in isolation depending on available moisture. Look for them late spring to early fall. Some people do not like the briny taste of this mushroom while others say it's fantastic. *A. bitorquis* looks similar, just smaller, less reddish, with a double ring and no salty smell.

Meadow Mushroom. These actually grow in meadows (surprise!). CREDIT: JAMES CHELIN

MEADOW MUSHROOM, PINK BOTTOM
Agaricus campestris
by James Chelin, Jennifer Bell

Family: Agaricaceae

Ecology: Ubiquitous! This mushroom can be found at the lowest elevation in Colorado (3,300 feet) up to tree line. It will thrive in the suburbs, in the fields of farmers, and in wild forests under ponderosa pine. Summer to early fall.

Description: Generally among the smallest of all Agaricus, white and round. The gills are a pleasant pink color in youth, turning to brown later, and close and not attached to the stem. The stem is of average height. When young, you might see a small ring. Generally not staining, but occasionally a pinkish hue. The flesh texture is like soft sand giving. Very little discoloration except for a pinkish hue when sliced. The mycologists would describe the smell as fungoid, meaning it smells like a mushroom growing a little funky with age. The spore print is dark chocolate brown.

Edibility: Excellent.

Notes: Much smaller than other Agaricus. Sometimes just a few to gregarious depending on available moisture. They especially like higher elevation meadows where cattle have grazed. They can fruit over and over again with sufficient rainfall. David Arora (1986) says this delicious mushroom grows abundantly pretty much everywhere, but people are so afraid of wild fungi that they will drive right past them on their way to the supermarket . . . to buy mushrooms.

A. *xanthodermus* types and A. *arvensis* are the tricksters that can also be found growing commonly in the Rockies. Keep KOH in your backpack to help differentiate. Xanthodermus types are mildly poisonous and they announce themselves by staining a harsh yellow near the base and smelling nasty.

The Emperor Mushroom. These get big and are probably the best of the Agaricus. CREDIT: JAMES CHELIN

EMPEROR (formerly known as the Prince)
Agaricus julius
by James Chelin, Jennifer Bell

Family: Agaricaceae

Ecology: You can use your altimeter to find this mushroom as it loves high mountains and spruce. It appears from July to August in Colorado.

Description: The cap is large, and the coloring is similar to the portobello you find in stores except the julius has a scaled pattern on it, brown on tan, similar to lace stockings. It can turn slightly yellow where damaged or nicked. When young it has a cottony veil covering the gills. As it matures it becomes quite large and flattens. The gills are initially pinkish gray to pink when young then brown at maturity and crowded, not attached to the stem. The stem is tall and average to thick for the size of mushroom, changing in appearance with age from shaggy to smooth. Sometimes it is slightly curved—with a larger bulbous base. Once the cap unfurls it leaves a thin, yellowish to taupe skirt-like ring. When fully mature the stalk can turn dark above the ring. The flesh is white but can transform to a mellow yellow color when nicked. It has a very distinct and totally delightful cherry-almond aroma. The spore print is dark chocolate brown.

Edibility: Yumyumyum.

Notes: *A. julius* is the Rocky Mountain version of the Prince, or *A. augustus*, and is closely related to that fungus. It is a rarer, woodland Agaricus and is highly sought after by foragers who consider it the best tasting Agaricus for the pot. It can become fairly large and is often found in small groups.

Woodland Agaricus. This is actually a group of similar species. CREDIT: IAN FIERMAN

WOODLAND AGARICUS
Agaricus didymus
by James Chelin

Ecology: Woodland Agaricus can be found under conifers from the ponderosa pine belt up higher into the mountains under spruce. They prefer needle duff. Summer to early fall in Colorado.

Description: The caps are medium to large in size. They tend to stain yellow when bruised or handled, especially on the cap. The cap can crack with age especially when moisture dries up. The veils have a classic cogwheel pattern when young. The gills are initially white to pinkish gray when young then turn brown fairly quickly at maturity, crowded, not attached to the stem. The stem is usually tall with a skirt-like ring and generally with a bulbous base. The flesh is white at first. The flesh stains yellow in fresh specimens where nicked or handled on the edges of the cap. Some such as *A. didymus* can turn a distinct golden color with age. The smell is of anise or almond. The spore print is dark chocolate brown.

Edibility: Edible.

Notes: Yellow-staining woodland Agaricus varieties are somewhat common. We have several similar related mushrooms in the Rocky Mountains. They are closely related to our city-dwelling *Agaricus arvensis*. Some of them remain undescribed and are unknown. They have always been referred to as *Agaricus sylvicola* in most literature. *A. sylvicola*, however, is a close relative that is found on the West Coast.

A. didymus is one of the most common and abundant. The color starts out white, stains yellow on the edges, and turns to a nice golden color with age. Sometimes some slight cracking on the cap depending on moisture. It usually has a curved, large bulbous base, which is a key feature. It has a strong aroma of cherry-almond. It is very common under ponderosa pine and spruce. They cook up to a nice golden yellow color. They also go great on a pizza!

Agaricus gemellatus is a little larger with a slightly bulb-like base that is straight rather than curved. It is difficult to identify with 100% certainty as there isn't much information about this particular species.

Agaricus mesocarpus ages to a golden color much like *A. didymus*. It is the smaller of the woodland Agaricus and it is difficult to tell the difference from macroscopic features.

Shaggy Parasol. Common in towns, but be sure you don't have the poisonous green-gilled mushroom.
CREDIT: JAMES CHELIN

SHAGGY PARASOL
Chlorophyllum rachodes
by James Chelin and Jennifer Bell

Family: Agaricaceae

Ecology: Find these fungi in the foothill areas of Colorado growing on the ground under gambel oak and ponderosa pine. They are fairly common early summer through fall and typically grow in small, scattered groups.

Description: This large fungus starts out perfectly round, similar to a baseball with brown warts. As it ages it unfurls into a large umbrella-like cap. It changes from white to cinnamon brown as it ages. The white gills are broad and unattached to the stem, turning brown with age. The stem is stiff and hard—more like a tree branch than a mushroom stem. Has a basal bulb and a thick double-edged ring. The flesh is of medium consistency. All parts of the mushroom turn reddish brown with handling and age. The aroma is similar to that of the mushrooms you buy at the store. The spore print is white.

Shaggy Parasol. These often grow in large groups, but usually not in grass. CREDIT: IKUKO LUBOW

Edibility: Yum.

Notes: There are other parasol mushrooms like *Chlorophyllum brunneum*. Spores are white in this one as well, and it is also edible. The smaller ring can help you to differentiate.

Here is a great opportunity to learn how to do a spore print. The shaggy parasol throws white spores and is quite delicious. *Chlorophyllum molybdites* looks VERY similar but has green spores on paper and also fruits earlier in the year on lawns. *Lepiota magnispora* looks similar as well, but is much smaller and likes higher altitudes. It is also poisonous.

RECIPE

Double Agaricus Pho

BY JENNIFER BELL

Ingredients
1 handful fresh Agaricus mushrooms
1 handful dried Agaricus mushrooms
Bag of beef bones from your favorite butcher
1 carrot diced
1 carrot sliced
2 celery sticks diced
1 medium-sized sweet onion
3 garlic cloves
1 bunch scallions
1 bunch radishes or 1 daikon radish
1 head cabbage or bok choy
1 small piece ginger
A few pieces kombu
1 teaspoon bonito flakes
2 packages soba noodles
1 teaspoon herbs de provence
1 large pinch parsley
2 bay leaves
Water (enough to almost fill the pot)
Oil for frying

Double Agaricus Pho Broth.
CREDIT: JENNIFER BELL

Preparation
1. Heat the oven to 375° F.
2. Put the bones on a baking sheet along with your mushroom lover's mirepoix: sweet onions, carrots, celery, garlic, and dried Agaricus. Any kind of Agaricus will do. Add herbs de provence and parsley.
3. Roast until browned and caramelized.
4. Put everything in a large pot with a bay leaf or two, add water, and simmer on the stove (with a tight cover) for a day or two.
5. Strain the broth. Freeze some for later in unsealed plastic containers. The fat will rise to the top. You can toss this if you're on a diet or keep it to saute the vegetables for the pho.
6. Add the scallions, carrots, radishes, daikons, and cabbage or bok choy. Now bring out fresh Agaricus and fry lightly in oil—so the mushroom is cooked but not soft. Don't add salt as it causes the fungus to steam and get mushy.
7. Heat some of the stock in a saucepan. Add grated ginger, kombu, and bonito flakes. Strain again. Add soba noodles. When the noodles are almost done add the vegetables you prepared, and the mushrooms.

12. Amanita

An edible Grisette. CREDIT: PATRICIA BUKUR

Amanita is a large genus of mushrooms that have gills not attached to the stem, white spore prints, and either a stem a cup-like feature at the base of the stem or the base that is like a bulb.

Although there are edible Amanita species, they should be treated with great caution for eating. **Amanitas kill more people than all other mushroom groups put together. Be absolutely certain that any Amanita you plan to eat has been correctly identified.**

The saclike structure around the base of the stem is called a "volva." CREDIT: JOSEPH O'HALLARON

GRISETTES
Amanita vaginata group

by Patricia Bukur and Ian Fierman

Amanita in section *Vaginatae* are a group of edible mushrooms that are loosely termed Grisettes. They are within the family Amanitaceae, which is composed of the genus *Amanita,* as well as some smaller genera like Catatrama, Limacella, and three or four others, depending on which expert you ask.

Amanita vaginata is considered the prototype species for this group, which has the general features of a striated cap, free white gills, a stem with a saclike volva housing a non-bulbous base, and no ring. According to Bunyard and Justice (2020) *Amanita* sect. *Vaginatae* is the largest subgenus of Amanita with about 300 taxa worldwide and many poorly identified species as well as those under taxonomic review. Originally, these mushrooms were lumped into the same category as Amanita *Caesareae* due to some superficial similarities but differentiation is far more clear today, as those in section *Vaginatae* are not brightly colored like the Caesars and have stalks without a ring. Recent DNA analysis has shown that the two sections are not as closely related as once believed. Other than both belonging to the genus *Amanita,* the only real similarity between the *Vaginatae* and the *Caesareae* is that all mushrooms contained in both of those sections are considered edible.

Mushrooms in this group have saclike, or occasionally somewhat cuplike volvas, but they lack a ring on the stem and don't have the bulbous base or warts on the cap found on some other species of Amanita, such as *A. muscaria*. This genus contains some species that are deadly toxic, while others are considered choice edibles, and knowing the features of every group is immensely helpful because mushrooms in certain sections of the genus are all considered edible, while mushrooms in other sections are considered toxic. The *A. vaginata* group are well-known and delicious mushrooms and our Grisettes found in the Rocky Mountains are no exception to this statement.

There are two main morphological types of *A. vaginata* based on the appearance of the universal veil: One has a persistent membranous saccate volva and is usually gray or brown, and the other has a universal veil composed of non-membranous tissue that appears as broken patches or flattened warts on the cap and stalk base. All Amanita species in this section have a negative reaction to Melzer's reagent, meaning that spores do not turn blue, black, or brick red when the solution is applied. Stalks are generally white or grayish and the base has a fragile, loose sac. They are not to be confused with Amanita species in subsection *Pantherinae*, aka "panther caps," which have a ring on the stem, cuplike instead of a saclike volva, and a cap that ranges from brownish to silver, usually with warts from the breaking of the universal veil.

In the Southern Rocky Mountains we have a handful of Grisettes that the forager may encounter from the lower elevation riparian areas to the dense conifer forests of the subalpine zones.

Grisette. CREDIT: RON WOLF

Poplar-Loving Amanita. These usually come up around the end of June in the Denver area under cottonwoods. CREDIT: IAN FIERMAN

POPLAR-LOVING AMANITA
Amanita populiphila

Family: Amanitaceae

Ecology: Late spring and summer from 5,000 to 9,500 feet, from plains to montane zones. At lower elevations, these mushrooms are commonly encountered in riparian areas near cottonwood, especially on slightly raised grassy areas around drainage ditches and other places considered prone to flooding. Occasionally growing singularly, but more often fruiting in groups or sometimes large clusters of dozens and occasionally even hundreds!

Description: The cap is small to medium sized and oval or bell-shaped at first, becoming flat with a lump (umbo) in the middle, eventually with an uplifted margin at maturity. It is off-white or pale cream, turning straw-colored, tan, or light brown with age. The poplar-loving Amanita is usually speckled with whitish remnants of the universal veil, sometimes visible as thicker warts or smooth little patches. The surface is sticky when moist and slippery when wet. The cap margin is striated on the edge, often faintly so at first, eventually spreading to about 40% of the cap's radius.

The gills are narrowly attached or free from the stem and they are off-white to cream with rosy pink to pale orange hues, often with woolly material near the marginal edge that can be tinted blush or pale orange and turns yellowish orange or peachy in dried specimens. Like all of our Grisettes, it lacks a ring (exannulate). The stem is relatively thin and fragile and is either hollow or stuffed. It is off-white in color, sometimes with pallid watery streaks and the upper surface is usually adorned with pale orange floccules. The volva is slightly membranous and white, but commonly discolors reddish orange, bronze, or brown. It is quite fragile, often falls apart into small chunks, easily detaches from the stem, and is often difficult to excavate without fracturing or snapping off entirely. The odor of this mushroom is mild and faintly pleasant but it can develop a fishy smell with age. Spores are white. **Edibility:** Edible and quite nice.

Notes: *A. populiphila* are mushrooms that get every forager excited because they are the earliest of the Grisettes. *Populiphila* for its tree hosts being of the genus *Populus* (poplar). At higher elevations they are less picky and can be found growing with other poplars like aspen. It has also been reported with *Salix* (willow), which is the sister genus to *Populus* in the family Salicaceae.

Barrows' Amanita. Notice the orange color inside the cup at the base of the stem. CREDIT: IAN FIERMAN

BARROWS' (RINGLESS) AMANITA
Amanita barrowsii

Family: Amanitaceae

Ecology: Found from July to September. Usually scattered individually over a broad area but occasionally fruiting gregariously with a tendency to grow in more open forests of aspen stands or mixed woods with aspen trees in upper-montane to subalpine zones. Common in some regions (e.g., Northern Colorado).

Description: The medium- to large-sized caps are orange, apricot, pinkish orange or pale orange-gold and bell-shaped at first (campanulate), becoming broadly campanulate to somewhat plane with a slight umbo (hump in center). The surface is slimy (viscid) when wet and lustrous when dry. *A. barrowsii* has a margin that is only faintly striated with lines on just 10% of the cap's radius. Its universal veil is usually absent or very infrequently displayed as a singular white patch on the orange cap. The gills are close, free from the stem. They are white with a light orange tinge and paler on the marginal edges, becoming pale ochre to burnt orange when dry. The stem lacks an annulus and is pallid to buff colored. The shape of the stem is nearly columnal, but usually tapers where it meets the cap (apex). The surface is sometimes scruffy and often has cream to orangish floccules near the apex. The volva is thick and tough, white on the outside and pale orange on the inside. They smell faintly fungal and pleasant, and according to Chuck Barrows, the fresh mushroom tastes sweet at first, then bitter. Spores are white.

Edibility: Delicious! Somewhat nutty and often quite sweet. They are underappreciated simply because they are barely known.

Notes: This fairly unmistakable mushroom can sometimes be found speckled throughout tall grass in vast expanses of open woods, and it is frequently growing adjacent to *Amanita stannea*, the tin cap Amanita. Rod Tulloss has hypothesized that *Amanita americrocea*, which has been occasionally sighted in the Rocky Mountains, might just be the same mushroom in another form with a different applied name, but currently *A. barrowsii* is considered endemic to the Southwest and is common in Colorado. The often impressively large saccate volva, lack of annulus, orangish cap, and tendency to grow with aspen trees are good characteristics for identification.

Amanita populiphila can look somewhat similar, but its cap is whitish to tan, the volva is quite fragile and sometimes stains rusty reddish orange or brown, and it is more often found growing at much lower elevations under cottonwood in riparian areas.

Tin Cap Amanita. The cap almost looks metallic on these. CREDIT: IKUKO LUBOW

TIN CAP AMANITA
Amanita 'stannea'

Family: Amanitaceae

Ecology: Found from July through early fall in aspen forests or mixed woods of conifers and aspen trees from lower montane to subalpine zones.

Description: Caps of this medium-sized, silver-colored Grisette are rounded, becoming more plane with an umbo as they mature. The cap's edge is lined with striations on about 30% of the radius, and it is covered in white patches of remnants from the volva that eventually turn more of a dirty orange color as the mushroom ages. Gills of this mushroom are crowded, free from the stem, and white, aging to a dull brownish at the marginal edges. The cylindrical stem lacks a ring and it is white with grayish fibers. A cup-like basal volva forms from the crumbly, thick universal veil and is whitish but is occasionally stained orange like the cap remnants. There is no noticeable odor and the spores are white.

Notes: This distinct, silver-capped Amanita is thought to be mycorrhizal with aspen trees, so the elevation range of *A. stannea* in the Southern Rocky Mountains could be about 7,000–11,000 feet, as they seem to start in lower montane forests and follow up to as high as aspen will grow into the lower alpine zones.

Grisette Frittata with Herbs and Goat Cheese

BY PATRICIA BUKUR

Ingredients

10 ounces fresh grisettes, gently washed to remove dirt, and sliced

3 tablespoons butter

2 tablespoons extra virgin olive oil

½ small onion diced

1 cup mixed, washed, and chopped vegetables such as spinach, kale, asparagus, bell peppers

1 handful chopped fresh herbs such as basil, thyme, and rosemary

Sea salt and freshly ground pepper

Cayenne

8 eggs, preferably cage-free

Goat cheese (soft) crumbled into large chunks

¼ cup grated aged parmesan

Preparation

1. Melt butter in a well-seasoned cast iron pan on medium heat, but be careful not to burn it. Add the onion, salt, and pepper, and cook for 3–5 minutes until soft. Add the chopped vegetables, raise the heat, and cook for about 5 minutes, stirring occasionally until they soften. Add the mushrooms and chopped herbs and cook for another 5–7 minutes. Adjust the salt and pepper as needed.
2. While the vegetables are cooking, beat eggs with some salt and pepper and a dash of cayenne. Pour evenly over vegetables and cover with a transparent lid. Cook undisturbed until eggs are still undercooked in the center, add goat cheese pieces, drizzle with olive oil, and place the pan under broiler for 1 minute.
3. Cut frittata into wedges, sprinkle with grated parmesan, and serve warm or at room temperature.

This frittata is perfect for a late breakfast or brunch. It's great with toasted seed bread or sourdough and lemon/olive oil green salad on the side. If you've been mushroom hunting and are exceptionally hungry, it pairs well with pan-roasted rosemary potatoes.

Grisettes are delicious, so if you are lucky to find them while foraging, enjoy cooking them the same day with beautiful herbs and vegetables that bring out their flavor. Have fun and bon appetit.

13. Tricholomas and Similar

A group of blewits. CREDIT: RON WOLF

As a group, these are cap and stem mushrooms with gills that are attached to the stem and produce white spore prints.

There are a few sought-after members, but there are several poisonous species and many of them are difficult to identify. Other than a few relatively easy to identify species they should be avoided.

Matsutake. One of the more sought after mushrooms. CREDIT: JOSEPH O'HALLARON

Matsutake. This button was growing alongside the mature mushroom that was barely starting to push up through the soil. CREDIT: IKUKO LUBOW

MATSUTAKE, WESTERN NORTH AMERICAN MATSUTAKE
Tricholoma murrillianum
by Miyako Boyett

Family: Tricholomataceae

Ecology: Late July through September, montane to subalpine, between 8,000 and 11,000 feet. Primarily associated with old growth lodgepole pine and subalpine fir. Growing alone, scattered, gregariously and occasionally forming a fairy ring in grayish sandy soil called podzol. Finding matsutake can be very challenging as they are often covered in thick pine needle duff. One must train their eye to spot a "mush lump" or "shlump"—slight rise in the vast pine needle duff.

Description: Caps medium to large, convex, and margin inrolled when young, becoming broadly convex or nearly flat with age, ivory white often with orangish brown streaks, flattened fibrils and small scales. Gills attached to the stem, close; short gills frequent, white to ivory, sometimes becoming brown or reddish brown with age, covered by a thick white cottony partial veil when young. Stalk short or average length, average thickness, firm and sturdy, slightly tapering to base, white above the ring, streaked orangish brown below;

False Matsutake. These grow at the same time and in the same places as matsutake, but they lack the odor and are more orange than matsutake. CREDIT: IAN FIERMAN

partial veil white and thick, collapsing to form a sheath around the lower stem and a prominent flaring ring at the top edge of the sheath. Odor of cinnamon, spicey, Red Hots, or dirty gym socks. The spore print is white.

Edibilty: Edible and choice.

Notes: Matsutake have been the most prized mushrooms in Japan for centuries and popular in the Western world for many years. The Japanese word *matsutake* translates to "pine mushroom" in English and they grow with (red) pines in Japan, as the name suggests. They have a very distinctive odor which is generally described as "fragrant pine" in Japan while "Red Hots" or "dirty gym socks" in the Western world. Anyone who was born and raised in Japan knows this odor by heart and our local Japanese foragers can often sense the smell before spotting the actual mushroom. There is almost nothing else in the world that smells like it, and you should be able to easily identify this mushroom by its odor once you become familiar with it. *Catathelasma ventricosum, Tricholoma focale,* and *Tricholoma dulciolens* (formerly called *Tricholoma caligatum*) are similar species.

Poplar Trich. These are often so covered in sand that they must be soaked for hours to remove it.
CREDIT: MIYAKO BOYETT

SAND MUSHROOM, POPLAR TRICH
Tricholoma populinum
by Miyako Boyett

Family: Tricholomataceae

Ecology: October through November, primarily in cottonwood riparian areas around 5,000 feet and up. Growing abundantly and usually in a large cluster, occasionally forming a fairy ring, halfway buried in loose sandy soil under deep cottonwood leaf litter, which may or may not appear as "mush lump" or "shlump."

Description: Caps 6–15 centimeters across, broad, conical, sometimes with low knob, margin inrolled when young, irregular and wavy when mature. Pinkish buff to dingy reddish brown in center and whitish toward margin. Gills close or crowded, whitish, sometimes with reddish brown spots, narrowly attached or notched. Stalks 5–10 centimeters long x 1.5–3 centimeters wide, solid and stocky, equal or narrowing or enlarging toward base, no ring. Flesh thick and solid, doesn't stain when cut. Be sure that the only trees nearby are cottonwoods, as there are very similar mushrooms that will grow only with other trees. The smell is farinaceous or cucumber-like. The spore print color is white.

Edibility: Edible and good.

Notes: The Sand mushroom is considered our season-ending mushroom, and it fruits in mid- to late fall in the lower elevations. They are generally underrated and underappreciated perhaps because they can be difficult to find. Deer favor this mushroom also, and oftentimes halfway consumed mushrooms are scattered on the ground, which may be the easiest way to find them.

There are some very similar Tricholoma species that are poisonous. To avoid the poisonous species, be certain that the only trees anywhere near are cottonwoods.

Similar mushrooms include *Hebeloma* spp., *Cortinarius* spp., and several poisonous Tricholoma species.

Man on Horseback. These are tougher to identify, so get help the first few times.

MAN ON HORSEBACK, YELLOW KNIGHT, CANARY TRICH
Tricholoma equestre group (=*T. flavovirens*)
by Patricia Bukur

Family: Tricholomataceae

Ecology: Typically from August until the aspen leaves fall, on the ground under pines.

Description: The fruiting bodies are conical with medium to large caps (up to 5 inches in diameter), flattened or wavy on maturity, sulfur or lemon colored, sticky, notched, with yellow gills. Upon maturity, brownish red streaking can be observed. Stalk is of average height and thickness, pale yellow or white, and fibrous. Spore prints are white. *T. equestre* tastes mild and mealy with little odor.

Notes: *T. equestre* is small- to medium-sized with an average-sized stem for the mushrooms of the genus *Tricholoma*. This species is found abundantly across North America and Europe in July and August. Found frequently in soil under pines, and sometimes under aspen trees, in Colorado and Wyoming. While it was once considered a choice edible, *T. equestre* (=*flavovirens*) is no longer recommended as forageable in North America due to deadly poisonings traced to the European species (specifically in France).

Mock Matsutake. The two rings on the stem are distinctive. Once the cap opens there will be a ring on both sides of the smooth area just below the cap.

MOCK MATSUTAKE, SWOLLEN-STALKED CAT
Catathelasma ventricosum
by Patricia Bukur

Family: Tricholomataceae
Ecology: Fruiting bodies are generally found under conifers in the Rocky Mountains between August and September.
Description: The fruiting body is medium-sized in diameter, largely convex, with firm flesh and white decurrent gills. Its look-alike, *Catathelasma imperiale* (matsutake), is larger and is

more white to brown capped rather than grayish. Stalks of *C. ventricosum* have two veils—the upper is white, and the lower is ochre-colored. The flesh is thick and hard, the taste is not pleasant, and the smell is mild but *not spicy* like matsutake. Catathelasma produces a white spore print with spores that are elliptical and smooth.

Edibility: Not poisonous. Edible if well cooked.

Notes: *C. ventricosum* is a heavy, dry-capped fungus with the common name mock matsutake. Catathelasma is very heavy, large, off-white, or grayish caps. It is distinguished from the prized matsutake by its very hard flesh, double veils, lack of spicy odor, and decurrent gills. Stains white.

Honey Mushrooms. Although this photo shows only a few separated mushrooms, these are often in huge clusters.

HONEY MUSHROOM
Armillaria solidipes (= *A. ostoyae*)
by Dr. Alex Cauley

Family: Physalacriaceae

Ecology: Appearing from late summer to fall, these mushrooms are typically found growing on roots, stumps, and at the base of trees. Although commonly associated with conifers, they can also be found on hardwoods. They often grow in dense clusters.

Description: Caps are small to medium in size. In younger specimens, the cap is usually convex or hemispherical in shape, presenting a rounded or dome-like appearance. As the mushroom matures, the cap flattens out and may also develop a central depression or become somewhat uplifted at the margin. The cap's margin sometimes develops striations (brief radial lines at its edges). The honey mushroom is named for its color rather than its flavor, with the surface of the cap appearing creamy gold to reddish brown, featuring darker, distinct scales that become less visible upon maturity. The cap's center is generally darker. To the touch, the cap can feel dry or slightly damp. Its flesh is white and firm without any significant color changes when exposed. With age, the flesh may become pinkish brown. Gills

A nice cluster of honey mushrooms. CREDIT: RON WOLF

range from white to cream, are moderately crowded, and are attached to the stalk, sometimes slightly decurrent (descending on the stalk). The stalk is typically cylindrical, maintaining a consistent width from top to bottom, and is adorned with a prominent annulus—a fleshy ring typically situated near the top. The stalk may exhibit either a straight or bent posture, and its color often mirrors the cap's surface, with possibly lighter or whitish shades. The odor can range from indistinct to mild, sometimes carrying hints of the forest floor.

Edibility: Considered edible when *thoroughly* cooked; otherwise, these mushrooms are unsafe to eat in their raw state. Even after cooking, it is advisable to exercise caution as some individuals may experience adverse reactions leading to gastrointestinal discomfort. To ensure safe tolerance, it is recommended to initially consume a smaller portion. The perceived flavor varies between people, with some detecting a somewhat sweet taste while others experience a mild to slightly bitter flavor.

Notes: These fungi demonstrate both saprobic and parasitic tendencies, leading to a condition known as Armillaria root disease, which causes the roots of affected trees to rot. Consequently, the infected trees become more vulnerable to stressors, and their weakened roots can lead to mortality due to the mechanical failure of the living tree. Notably, this fungus also holds the record for being one of the largest and oldest living organisms on Earth. A massive colony of this fungus was discovered in the Malheur National Forest in Oregon, which covers an estimated area of 2,200 acres and is believed to be at least 2,400 years old (R. Maheshwari, "The largest and oldest living organism," *Resonance*, vol. 10, pp. 4–9, 2005).

Velvet Foot. The stem is always velvety, an important identification feature.

ASPEN ENOKI
Flammulina populicola

VELVET FOOT, VELVET SHANK, WINTER MUSHROOM, ENOKITAKE
Flammulina velutipes
by Ian Fierman and Miyako Boyett

Ecology: July through August typically above 8,000 feet in mixed forest where aspen is present. *F. populicola* grows from the stumps, logs, roots and living wood of aspen, mostly in clusters but sometimes growing alone, scattered or gregariously. *F. velutipes* is less picky and will grow from any hardwood.

Description: Caps small to medium, convex when young, becoming broadly convex to flat, sticky when moist, golden to orangish brown in the center and cream to pale yellow toward the margin. Gills attached to the stalk, whitish to pale yellow, crowded or close. Stalk average to tall in height, average to slender in thickness, no ring, similar color to the cap margin above, darkening from the base upward to a dark brown, velvety in texture, fibrous and woody, equal or slightly tapered toward base. Does not bruise or stain when cut. The odor and flavor are mild. The spore print color is white.

Edibility: Edible and excellent.

Notes: Enoki are a good edible mushroom but often overlooked and underappreciated because they are not as commonly or abundantly found in our region and can be tricky for beginners to identify. However, they have been cultivated and enjoyed in Asian countries for many decades. Cultivated enoki are white, tall, and skinny with small caps while wild enoki look totally different.

Galerina marginata and various Gymnopus species can be very similar looking. Be sure to check that the stem is velvety.

Fairy Ring Mushroom. The stem is so tough that you can sometimes tie a knot with it. CREDIT: IKUKO LUBOW

FAIRY RING MUSHROOM
Marasmius oreades Fr.
by Saadia Naiman

Family: Marasmiaceae

Ecology: May through September. Common and widely distributed in lawns and other grassy areas forming rings or arcs growing close together or in clusters.

Description: Small in size, cap is smooth rounded or bell-shaped when young with a slightly darker incurved edge. Cap color can vary and ranges from caramel to light tan to pale beige or buff and when wet can be slightly translucent with faint edge striations. With advanced age, high sun exposure, and dryness, cap color will become a light beige or a pale buff. As aging occurs the cap shape becomes convex to broadly plane with the presence of an umbo or central bump that can be slightly darker. The edge may uplift and take on an uneven or wavy appearance. Gills are pale and cream colored and produce white spores. The gills are closer when young and become widely spaced and broad with age. Gills are free from stalk or attached and will *not* run down the stalk or be decurrent. Stalk is thin, straight, tough, resistant to breakage, and is equal in size from top to base, lighter in color near the top and darker and fuzzy closer to the base. Odor is mild (slight almond scent) and taste mild.

Edibility: Edible and excellent (caps only).

Because this species tends to grow exclusively in grassy areas and can be found in lawns, parks, golf courses, and urban settings where grasses can often be treated with herbicides or other harmful chemicals, it is important to forage specimens for the table in areas that have *not* been treated with chemicals or are highly polluted. An indication that an area may not have been treated with chemicals would be the presence of healthy weeds.

Note: Dried-out *M. oreades* when rehydrated can be "resurrected" or brought back to life with the capacity to yet again produce spores, making it a unique feature of this mushroom. The ability of this fungi to be revived makes it an excellent mushroom that can be dried, stored, and used for cooking at a later time.

Young Blewits. Young ones showing their typical lilac colors. CREDIT: RON WOLF

BLEWIT
Clitocybe nuda
by Natalie Hyde

Family: Tricholomataceae

Ecology: Appearing from late summer to early fall. *C. nuda* is commonly found growing on piles of debris. The saprobic fungi can be seen alone, scattered or in clusters in rich humus. In Colorado *C. nuda* is more commonly found in urban areas, grasslands, or woods. *C. nuda* is widespread across Europe and North America. It has been reported in Asia and South America and was first described in France.

Description: Cap is small to large with enrolled wavy margins that can develop with age. The most prominent feature of this species is its lilac purple colors on its cap, gills, and stem. This color may change with freshness. With age the purple hues within the flesh will turn a brown-buff pigmentation. This species lacks a partial veil (ring), as is present on the stem of other closely related mushrooms. Spore prints appear a pale pinkish color. Gills are attached to the stem and crowded. The gills also may have a light purple to white pigment. The stem is thick and may be enlarged at the base. Odor is distinctively sweet, some may describe it comparable to orange juice.

Older Blewit. When older the lilac colors fade. CREDIT: RON WOLF

Edibility: Considered edible when properly cooked, but considered unsafe to eat in their raw state. Considered good by some, but may lack in texture. It is advised to start with a small portion when consuming the species for the first time, as it can cause negative side effects such as gastrointestinal distress in some.

Notes: *C. nuda* can also be referred to as *Lepista nuda*. There is an ongoing debate on the proper taxonomy of *Clitocybe* (*Lepista*) *nuda* based on spore differences. This topic can be referenced on mushroomexpert.com.

Not a blewit. This is one of several Cortinarius species that can look very much like blewits.
CREDIT: ALEXIS MURRAY

Yep, not a blewit. Cortinarius can usually be identified by the rusty band near the top of the stem. CREDIT: ALEXIS MURRAY

Matsutake Soup

BY JAMES CHELIN

Time: About 45 minutes

Serves: 2 to 3 people

Ingredients
A couple of matsutake mushrooms
Spinach or baby kale leaves
Chives
Organic soy sauce
Sesame oil
Lime or lemon
Sea salt (optional)

Mushroom Stock
A handful dried mushrooms—boletes, Agaricus, shiitake, or others. A mixture works great!
A few slices ginger
⅓ medium onion
1 garlic clove
4 cups water
3 tablespoons organic soy sauce (approx.)
Sea salt

Preparation
The Stock
1. Bring the water to a boil in a pot. Add the stock ingredients except for the soy sauce and salt; then cook for at least 20 to 30 minutes.
2. Add a little bit of the soy sauce and sea salt.
3. Reduce the heat and simmer on low while you prepare the other ingredients.

The Mushrooms
1. Clean your mushrooms to remove any dirt.
2. Slice your mushrooms fairly thin about ⅛ inch or so.

3. Place them on a plate and drizzle with a little bit of sesame oil, a squeeze of lime or lemon, about a tablespoon or less of soy sauce and mix together well.
4. Sear the mushrooms quickly on both sides using a preheated pan. Cast iron works well.
5. Place a few spinach or baby kale leaves into 2 or 3 bowls.
6. Taste the mushroom stock again to see if it needs any soy sauce or salt and adjust accordingly.
7. Strain the hot stock into each bowl.
8. Place the mushroom slices on top.
9. Garnish with chives.
10. Enjoy!

Matsutake Soup. CREDIT: JAMES CHELIN

RECIPE

Sukiyaki with Matsutake

BY IKUKO LUBOW

Ingredients

½ cup soy sauce

2 tablespoons sugar

¼ cup sake

1 pound thinly sliced ribeye roast

2 to 3 green onions/leeks

½ shiitake

1 packet white enoki

2 packs shirataki/itogonnyaku (string yam)

½ matsutake

1 egg per person (optional)

Although matsutake is not commonly used in sukiyaki in Japan, due to the cost and availability, using matsutake enhances the flavor of this dish.

Preparation

1. Mix soy sauce, sugar, and sake in a small bowl.
2. Cook the remaining ingredients in a shallow pot while pouring the sauce over them.

It is common and popular to use raw egg to dip in, but some people may have concerns about *Salmonella* poisoning (I have never had a problem with it). Serve with steamed rice. Enjoy!

14. Oyster Mushrooms

Oyster Mushrooms. CREDIT: MAIA REED

by Orion Aon

Oyster mushrooms are saprotrophic, breaking down and digesting organic matter for nutrients. This trait makes them one of the world's most commonly cultivated mushrooms and one of the most common and easy-to-identify wild edible mushrooms in the Southern Rocky Mountains. Here, oyster mushrooms prefer decomposing wood from trees in the *Populus* genus, which includes cottonwoods, poplars, and aspens.

In Colorado and the Southern Rocky Mountains, we have two common species of oyster mushrooms and two that have reportedly been found but are rare. In the low to mid-elevations, the lung oyster *Pleurotus pulmonarius* can be found late winter through spring, fruiting from dead and dying cottonwoods and other deciduous species. In the mountains, aspen oysters, *P. populinus,* can be found fruiting from the wood of dead and dying aspens. The other two species are the pearl oyster mushroom, *P. ostreatus,* and the golden oyster, *P. citrinopileatus.* The first is a native species more common in the Midwest and eastern states. The second is a species native to Asia that has escaped cultivation and naturalized in many parts of North America.

Oyster Mushroom. CREDIT: IKUKO LUBOW

LUNG OYSTER
Pleurotus pulmonarius

Family: Pleurotaceae

Ecology: Can be found in low to mid-elevations during the warm months but are most common in spring. Will fruit from many species of deciduous hardwood trees but are most common on dead or dying cottonwood trees in urban and riparian habitats.

Description: Lung- or fan-shaped medium to large caps in shelf-like clusters. The clusters can be from a few to a huge number of mushrooms. They have short, off-centered stems with gills that run far down along the stem. Slight fishy odor, also often has notes of anise. The flesh is white and does not bruise or stain. Their spore color is white to lilac.

Edibility: Edible, but can become a little tough at full maturity.

Aspen Oyster. Similar to the regular oyster mushrooms, but typically smaller and paler colored.
CREDIT: IAN FIERMAN

ASPEN OYSTER
Pleurotus populinus

Family: Pleurotaceae

Ecology: Only fruits from dead and dying trees in the *Populus* genus. Most often found in stands of quaking aspens in montane habitats, but can also fruit in lower elevations.

Description: Fan- or shell-shaped caps in shelf-like clusters. Off-centered stems with gills that run down the stem. Their odor is similar to other oyster species but often more strongly of anise. The flesh is white and does not bruise or stain, and the spore color is white.

Edibility: Edible, but become a little tough at full maturity.

RECIPE

Oyster Mushroom Chowder

BY ED LUBOW

Ingredients

½ pound fresh oyster mushrooms cut into bite-sized pieces
½ cup onion chopped finely
4 tablespoons butter
1 cup potato chopped
3 tablespoons flour
2 egg yolks beaten
2 cups milk
2 cups sour cream
¼ cup sherry
¼ teaspoon thyme
A little mace, chives, hot sauce
Salt and pepper to taste

Preparation

1. Saute the mushrooms and onions in butter until the onions are translucent.
2. Add potatoes and cook until tender, about 15 minutes.
3. Add the seasonings, and then slowly stir in the milk and bring to a boil.
4. Add the rest of the ingredients.

15. Deer Mushrooms

Deer Mushroom. These will always be growing from wood. CREDIT: IAN FIERMAN

by Ian Fierman

Pluteus is a genus within the order of *Agaricales*, which are saprophytic decomposers of dead wood with pinkish spore prints and no volva. These features make these mushrooms easy to identify to genus, but from there it can sometimes be difficult to get to species. This is partially due to the fact that *Pluteus* is generally understudied and could contain a lot of species or subspecies that have been put under an "umbrella name," simply based on having similar macromorphological features to the prototypical reference mushroom named some time in the past.

There are at least a handful of obscure and rarely observed species that the forager or enthusiast may occasionally stumble upon in this region. In this chapter are the two most commonly encountered of the *Pluteus* spp. in the southern Rockies.

Deer Mushroom. One of the very few mushrooms with a pink spore print that can be eaten safely.
CREDIT: IAN FIERMAN

DEER MUSHROOM, DEER SHIELD
Pluteus cervinus group

Family: Pluteaceae

Ecology: July to September in a wide range of ecosystems from the prairies to upper-montane zones. Usually growing singular or in a small group. Saprobic, growing on dead fallen hardwoods and can also be found on conifers, decomposing roots, buried wood, stumps, and sawdust or wood-chip piles.

Description: The cap is grayish brown to brown and conical to convex. It is smooth and silken to the touch and has a dark brown layer of thin hairs. Gills are close, not attached to the stem, and they are off-white at first, developing a pinkish hue with age. Stem is beige with brownish filaments and is cylindrical or tapered with a slightly larger base. There is no volva or ring present. The smell is somewhat earthy, metallic, or radish-like and the taste is mild. Spore print is a pale tan-pink.

Edibility: Edible and sometimes good, particularly when small.

Notes: This mushroom is fairly easy to identify if you aren't worried about being too specific. It is common in a sense, but misrepresented taxonomically in that there are several mushrooms which have had the name *P. cervinus* applied to them that probably aren't genetically the same as the *P. cervinus* first described. In most cases, this is probably a broad attempt to generalize things with a species that has an incomplete database and a lot of genetically similar look-alikes.

Pluteus petasatus is another commonly encountered mushroom in the genus and it is frustratingly similar at times, but it has a cap that is paler brown or whitish and usually scaly in the center. It often grows among sawdust and wood chips in urban areas, but is also frequently found in areas of woods affected by forest fires, particularly the first year or two after. It is also edible.

Melanoleuca species can be very similar to these, but they do not grow from wood, their gills are narrowly attached to the stem, and they will produce a white (not pinkish) spore print.

RECIPE

Basic Sauteed Mushrooms

BY ED LUBOW

Ingredients

Fresh mushrooms cut into bite-sized pieces

Olive oil (not virgin, since we're cooking with it here) or butter

Salt to taste

Optional Ingredients

Garlic

Ginger

Black pepper

Hot pepper

Parsley

Thyme

Preparation

1. Saute the mushrooms in a small amount of oil or butter.
2. Add salt to taste.

The whole point of this recipe is that it avoids adding much to the basic flavor of the mushroom other than a little salt. So this is a good way to use mushrooms with faint or subtle flavors, or to try a new mushroom to see what its basic flavor is so you can decide what sort of recipe might work well with it.

On the other hand, the optional ingredients are a few ideas for enhancing this recipe if all you want to do is have some sauteed mushrooms.

16. Poisonous Mushrooms

MUSHROOM POISONING

When eating wild mushrooms, there are many ways things can go wrong. If you become sick after eating mushrooms, SEEK MEDICAL ATTENTION IMMEDIATELY. In the most dangerous cases where the poisoning could result in death, medical treatment makes it 10 times as likely that you will survive (50% fatality rate down to 5%).

If eating wild mushrooms you or a friend have found, save some uncooked in the refrigerator overnight after the meal. If you become sick, these mushrooms can be shown to an expert to verify what you ate. In many cases this can help rule out the mushrooms as the cause of the illness.

The most common symptoms of mushroom poisoning are nausea, vomiting, abdominal cramping, and diarrhea. However, the exact symptoms for a poisoning will depend on which toxin(s) were consumed, along with other factors such as what they were consumed with or the health of the individual. The most common cause of mushroom poisoning is misidentification.

Misidentification

If there is any doubt about whether a mushroom is edible, DON'T EAT IT.

When comparing a mushroom you've found to a description of a species, every single bit of the description must match the found mushroom to be an accurate match. Beginning mushroom hunters are prone to overoptimism, stretching parts of a description "a little" (or even sometimes ignoring them) to make the mushroom match. Also, do not rely too much on comparing your find to photographs. Until you have experience, you may be ignoring features that are important and paying too much attention to things that are not.

Immigrants and foreign visitors can find mushrooms that look "just like" something they would find back where they learned mushroom hunting. This has been the cause of some of the most serious and tragic poisonings.

Do not assume that all mushrooms found in a group are the same kind. It is possible for poisonous and edible mushrooms to grow alongside each other. Examine each individual to verify that it is actually what you are trying to collect.

Overeating

Eating too much of anything will make you sick, and mushrooms are certainly not an exception. To avoid this, eat mushrooms in moderation.

Eating the same mushrooms several days in a row has resulted in some cases of poisoning. In these cases, there is a toxin that is harmless in the small amounts normally consumed. With toxins that can take several days to be eliminated from the body, eating those mushrooms many times over several days can result in illness. In particular this can be an issue with some medicinal mushrooms, especially when a mushroom extract or tincture is made and concentrated.

One fortunately rare possibility is intestinal obstruction. The majority of the bulk of a mushroom is indigestible fiber. In cases of excessive eating, there have been instances where the mass of fiber can form a plug that blocks the intestine. In severe cases surgery might be required to remove the blockage and avoid death.

Raw or Undercooked Mushrooms

Many edible mushrooms will make you sick if they are not thoroughly cooked. Honey mushrooms (*Armillaria* sp.) and morels (*Morchella* sp.) are especially notorious in this regard. Unless you specifically know that a particular kind of mushroom is edible raw, all wild mushrooms should be thoroughly cooked before eating. Note that in early 2023 there was a case of a restaurant serving raw/undercooked morels (depending on the date) where two of the poisoning victims died.

Bugs

One of the first things to do with a mushroom you have identified as an edible is to cut it to verify the absence of insect larvae. Almost all mushrooms are extremely popular with various insects that will then lay their eggs on them. These larvae will betray their presence by leaving tunnels through the flesh of the mushroom. Aside from the general undesirability of eating bugs, the issue is not so much eating the actual bugs but their feces which are left behind in those tunnels. That fecal material will very likely contain pathogenic bacteria that can cause serious illness.

Rot

Simply put, look at the mushroom you're considering eating and ask yourself if you would eat a piece of fruit or a vegetable in the same state. Do not eat any mushrooms that are visibly moldy, smell like they're rotting, or are becoming soft and discolored.

When collecting mushrooms, do not use plastic bags. The mushrooms will "sweat" inside these bags, and the extra moisture can promote rotting.

Contamination

Fungi can absorb toxic chemicals from their environment along with the nutrients they need to survive, potentially making an otherwise edible mushroom poisonous. One common potential source of toxins are the various weed-killing chemicals that are sprayed on some areas. Golf courses are particularly notorious in this regard. Another potential toxic environment is areas near mines, as the tailings can include many heavy metals.

Alcohol

There are some otherwise edible mushrooms that will make you sick if you consume alcohol. In some cases, individuals may be much more sensitive to this than most people. In particular, some people are sensitive to alcohol when eating morels (*Morchella* sp.) or king boletes (*Boletus* sp.).

Anxiety (Placebo Effect)
This crops up when someone has eaten a nontoxic mushroom but then worries excessively that they may have eaten something toxic. This is particularly a risk with small children that may have eaten a mushroom found in the yard or play area. The adults panicking can result in the child becoming ill because of the stress. In some of these cases, the child didn't even eat the mushroom—they only picked it up and had it in their hand.

Individual Reactions
Sometimes it is even possible to become sick when eating an edible mushroom. When trying a new kind of mushroom, eat only a small amount the first time. For example, many people cannot eat shiitake (*Lentinula edodes*) without breaking out into hives. With the kinds of mushrooms considered edible these reactions are rare, but they can happen with any kind of mushroom.

Drug Interactions
It is possible for medications you take to cause undesirable side effects when some mushrooms are eaten. For example, tree ears (*Auricularia* sp.) have an anticoagulant effect. There have been cases where a patient recovering from surgery has been brought food containing tree ears as an ingredient and they begin to bleed from the surgical site because their blood will not clot properly.

MUSHROOM TOXINS
Amatoxin
This causes more fatalities than all other mushroom toxins put together. As the name suggests, it was first discovered in mushrooms from the genus *Amanita*. Dangerous levels of this toxin occur in several other genera. Death usually occurs in 7–10 days from liver failure. Overall, the fatality rate for these poisonings is about 50% without medical treatment. If the victim receives medical treatment the survival rate improves to about 95%.
Genera: *Amanita, Galerina, Lepiota, Conocybe*

Orellanine
This toxin is noteworthy for having an extremely long delay before symptoms appear, up to three weeks. It permanently damages the kidneys and can cause death.
Genus: *Cortinarius*

Gyromitrin

Gyromitrin breaks down fairly readily into monomethylhydrazine, which is the true toxin. It takes the body several days to remove this toxin, so meals containing the toxin on consecutive days can result in the toxin building up to dangerous levels. Fortunately, death is rare from this poisoning.
Genus: *Gyromitra*

Muscarine

As the name suggests, this toxin was first discovered in *Amanita muscaria*, although it is not the main toxin in that mushroom. The onset of symptoms is very rapid compared to other toxins, typically within 15–30 minutes. Death is possible, but extremely rare.
Genera: *Inocybe, Clitocybe, Mycena*

Ibotenic Acid/Muscimole

These are the main toxins in *Amanita muscaria* and *Amanita pantherina*. Death is possible, but extremely rare.
Genus: *Amanita*

Psilocin

This is the toxin that produces the high of psychedelic mushrooms. Note that the effects on prepubescent children are very different and can be dangerous.
Genera: *Psilocybe, Panaeolus, Gymnopilus*

Coprine

This toxin produces effects when consumed with alcohol.
Genus: *Coprinopsis*

Gastrointestinal Irritants

This is a group of many different chemicals that have similar effects. The majority of mushroom poisonings are a result of this group. These produce the basic effects of most mushroom poisonings: nausea, vomiting, abdominal cramps, and diarrhea.

Other Toxins

Paxillus involutus is an uncommon mushroom that produces an autoimmune effect. Some people eat it without issue several times. When the toxic effect happens, the victim's immune system attacks their red blood cells, resulting in sudden acute anemia. This has caused some deaths in Europe and Asia.

Death Angel. Found under oak, these can become yellowish as they age. CREDIT: JENNIFER BELL

DEATH ANGEL
Amanita bisporigera

Family: Amanitaceae

Ecology: July, August, and September on the ground under oak, usually single or a few.

Description: This is a small to medium mushroom. The cap is smooth, usually without any warts, white, sometimes becoming tan then ocher colored in age. Gills free from the stem, close, white in color. Stem slender, usually tapering upward, with a fragile skirt-like ring near the top and a membranous saclike volva at the base, usually smooth, white.

Death Cap. Fortunately, this mushroom has not yet been found in Colorado. CREDIT: RON WOLF

Notes: Currently this is the only Amanita species with high amatoxin levels recorded from Colorado. *Amanita phalloides* is an invasive species originating in Europe that will probably be found here at some point in the future. It is similar in appearance to *A. bisporigera* but typically larger and usually has a brownish to greenish cap color.

Deadly Galerina. The galerina is the bigger mushroom with a ring; the rest are mycena. CREDIT: IAN FIERMAN

DEADLY GALERINA
Galerina marginata

Family: Hymenogastraceae

Ecology: June through September above 7,800 feet on dead wood or sometimes in moss, usually in clusters but sometimes only one or a few.

Description: These are small mushrooms, convex becoming flat, smooth, viscid to dry, ochraceous tawny fading to dull tan in color, hygrophanous. Gills attached to the stem, close to crowded, narrow, very pale brownish becoming tawny with age. Stem of moderate thickness and length, equal, whitish or pale brown at first becoming rusty brown, darker toward the base, with a conspicuous ring at first, the ring often becoming a ring zone or disappearing entirely.

Notes: This is very probably the most common deadly mushroom to be found in Colorado.

Deadly Galerina. They will rarely look this perfect.
CREDIT: RON WOLF

A common city Lepiota. CREDIT: IKUKO LUBOW

THE GENUS *LEPIOTA*

Family: Agaricaceae
Ecology: These grow in dead plant debris during the warm months, commonly in city habitats as well as in forests.
Description: These are small- to medium-sized mushrooms with convex to flat caps that are conspicuously scaly. The gills are free from the stem and white. The stem is slender to moderate in thickness, and often has a ring. All Lepiota species should be avoided, as many of them have dangerous levels of potentially deadly amatoxins.

A typical Cortinarius. Notice the rusty brown ring area on the stem. CREDIT: ALEXIS MURRAY

THE GENUS *CORTINARIUS*

Family: Cortinariaceae

Ecology: These are mycorrhizal associates with various tree species. Depending on altitude they might be found during any of the warm months of the year, but the majority will be found during the late summer mushroom season.

Description: *Cortinarius* is currently the largest genus of mushrooms, with more than 5,000 species. Identification to genus is mostly easy—they are small to large in size, the gills are attached to the stem, the spore print is a characteristic rusty brown color, and when young they have a partial veil that resembles a thick cobweb called a cortina, which is where the genus gets its name. In spite of the huge number of species, none of them found in the Rocky Mountain region are known to be any good to eat, and a few of them contain orellanine, which can kill by destroying the kidneys. Since they are very difficult to identify accurately to species, they should not be eaten.

False Morel. The cap is wrinkled instead of pitted like a morel.

FALSE MOREL, BRAIN MUSHROOM
Gyromitra esculenta

Family: Discinaceae

Ecology: Found in spring on the ground, usually under various conifers.

Description: These small- to medium-sized mushrooms are fairly easy to identify by their deeply folded and wrinkled brown to reddish brown to blackish in age caps that somewhat resemble a brain and a tan-colored stem that is not massive compared to the cap. There are no gills or teeth or tubes under the cap; in fact, the spores are produced from the outside surface of the cap.

Saddle-Shaped False Morel. Unlike other false morels, these grow in late summer on dead wood.
CREDIT: ALEXIS MURRAY

SADDLE-SHAPED FALSE MOREL
Gyromitra infula

Family: Discinaceae

Ecology: Found in late summer to fall on dead wood, although the wood can be buried so that they might appear to be growing on the ground.

Description: These are medium to large mushrooms that are easy to identify because they fruit long after most false morels, they almost always grow on dead wood, their reddish brown to dark brown cap is saddle shaped although it can sometimes have more than two lobes, and the stem is white to brownish and fairly cylindrical. As with other false morels, there are no gills, tubes, or teeth, and the spores are produced from the outside surface of the cap.

Ink Cap. CREDIT: JAMES LENTZ

INK CAP, ALCOHOL INK CAP
Coprinopsis atramentaria

Family: Psathyrellaceae

Ecology: Found during the warm months growing from dead wood or woody debris.

Description: The caps are medium sized, roughly egg shaped, and gray to tan, often with vertical lines. The stem is average to tall for the mushroom size, white, smooth or finely hairy, hollow, and with a subtle ring very near the base. The gills are white when young and so crowded that they almost look like a solid mass, but they soon turn black and become an ink-like slime that drips from the cap.

Notes: If consumed without alcohol they are edible, but not worth getting excited about. If any alcohol is consumed within two days before or up to three days after eating these, the person eating them will become very ill. The illness is not life threatening, but it is quite unpleasant.

Fly Agaric. These show up in art everywhere. Notice the multiple rings at the base of the stem.
CREDIT: IKUKO LUBOW

FLY AGARIC
Amanita muscaria

Family: Amanitaceae

Ecology: These are found in summer into fall on the ground with a variety of conifers with which it has a mycorrhizal association.

Description: This is probably the most recognizable mushroom you will ever find. The classic red-capped mushroom with whitish warts and a white stem with a ring toward the top and an enlarged base with multiple rings of tissue is widely portrayed in art and culture as the prototype of a mushroom. They are medium to large sized, and the cap can be other colors than red, especially as it fades, from red to orangish to yellow to tan to nearly white. Although the warts are usually white when the mushroom is mature, when it first comes up they are almost always a bright yellow color.

Notes: Although this mushroom should not be eaten, it commonly fruits at the same time and in the same places as the highly sought after king bolete (*Boletus rubriceps*). So if you find some of these easy to spot mushrooms you should probably start searching for the somewhat harder to find boletes.

Panther Cap. The main variety in this area has a pale cap. CREDIT: IKUKO LUBOW

PANTHER CAP
Amanita pantherina

Family: Amanitaceae

Ecology: These grow from the ground in late spring into summer with various conifers.

Description: Small to large but usually medium sized, these are usually among the earlier mushrooms of summer in the conifer forests. The most common variety has a very pale tan cap that is flat when mature, few or no warts, a slender stem with a ring above the middle, and a slightly bulbous base with a distinct ridge of tissue at the top of the bulb.

A typical Inocybe. These are even difficult to identify using a microscope.

THE GENUS *INOCYBE* (SENSU LATO)

Family: Inocybaceae

Ecology: These are mycorrhizal associates with various tree species. Depending on altitude they might be found during any of the warm months of the year, but the majority will be found during the late summer mushroom season.

Description: This is a large group of more than 1,000 species of little brown mushrooms (LBMs). They are mostly small mushrooms (a few might make it up to medium size) that are found associated with various trees. They tend to have a strikingly fibrous cap surface and this separates them from most other mushrooms. The gills are attached to the stem, and the spore print will be some shade of brown. Most of them grow on the ground, although there are a few that will be found on well-rotted stumps. Many of them have distinctive odors. They are notoriously difficult to identify accurately to species, even with a microscope.

Notes: None of them should be considered edible. Most of those studied for toxins contain dangerous levels of muscarine.

A typical Clitocybe.

THE GENUS *CLITOCYBE*

Family: Tricholomataceae

Ecology: These are saprotrophs, digesting dead plant debris, found from near snowbanks in spring up until the hard freezes.

Description: These are small- to medium-sized mushrooms with white to gray to brownish caps that are usually flat to somewhat funnel shaped. Most mushrooms you will find on the ground with pale gills that run down the stem will be members of this genus. Other than the members of the subgroup Lepista, which will be covered elsewhere, they should be avoided, as many of them, especially the whitish species, have high levels of muscarine.

Chlorophyllum molybdites. This mushroom causes more poisonings than any other in our region.
CREDIT: SAADIA NAIMAN

GREEN GILL, FALSE PARASOL MUSHROOM
Chlorophyllum molybdites

Family: Agaricaceae

Ecology: June through September in urban areas, most often in lawns.

Description: This is a large mushroom, medium when young, cap spherical or convex at first, becoming broadly convex to flat, whitish to tan, soon developing darker brown scales. Gills free, close, white, becoming dull greenish. Stem slender for the size of mushroom, white to brown, smooth, tapering upward, with a conspicuous double-edged movable ring, often bruising brownish, reddish, or pinkish, especially toward the base.

Notes: This mushroom causes more poisonings than any other mushroom in Colorado. It causes severe nausea, vomiting, abdominal cramping, and diarrhea usually 1 to 3 hours after consumption. It is very similar to the edible species *Chlorophyllum rachodes* and *Chlorophyllum brunneum*, from which it differs most easily by having a greenish spore print (the edible species have white spore prints).

The common poisonous Agaricus. Notice the bright yellow spot at the inside of the base of the stem.
CREDIT: IAN FIERMAN

YELLOW STAINER
Agaricus aff. *xanthodermus*

Family: Agaricaceae
Ecology: Urban lawns and parks along the front range in Colorado.
Description: This is a medium-sized white mushroom similar in appearance to the button mushroom sold in supermarkets. They generally have a long, curved stem that turns chrome yellow at the base when fresh. The stem is generally longer than the width of the cap at maturity, curved with a thick, felt-like ring. The cap is shaped at first like a deformed marshmallow—less circular, and forms a darker, depressed center. It smells unpleasant with a chemical odor similar to that of a chalkboard especially when a small piece is crushed. The smell of this mushroom is one of its key features. Unfortunately, not all people can smell the different odors of various Agaricus species. It can be easily confused with the edible *Agaricus arvensis*.

Sulfur Tuft. CREDIT: NICKLAUS WATSON

SULFUR TUFT
Hypholoma fasciculare (=Naematoloma fasciculare)

Family: Strophariaceae

Ecology: May through September on stumps, dead roots, and dead logs of both conifers and hardwoods, usually in large clusters. It has been found in the city of Denver as well as in the mountains.

Description: These are small mushrooms, the cap convex, becoming flat, yellow to greenish yellow when fresh but commonly orangish, reddish brown, brown, or whitish. The gills are attached to the stem, close to crowded, yellowish, becoming greenish yellow then dark purplish as the spores mature. The stem is narrow and of moderate to long size, equal or tapering somewhat downward, yellow, developing rusty brown coloration from the base

Please don't eat these. CREDIT: RON WOLF

upward. When young there is a yellow cortina, but this soon disappears or becomes a superior ring zone. It tastes bitter.

Notes: Eating this causes nausea, vomiting, and convulsions. A death in Europe has been attributed to this species, but it was consumed with other mushrooms in the same meal so it is possible that it was not the cause of death.

REFERENCES

Arora, David (1986). *Mushrooms Demystified.*
Evenson, Vera, and Denver Botanic Gardens (2015). *Mushrooms of Colorado and the Southern Rocky Mountains.*
Miller Jr., Orson K., and Miller, Hope (2006). *North American Mushrooms.*
Kerrigan, Richard (2016). *Agaricus of North America.*
Bunyard, Britt A., and Justice, Jay (2020). *Amanitas of North America.*

Chelin, James (2023). ColoradoMushrooms.com.
Kuo, Michael (2023). Mushroomexpert.com.
Wood, Michael (2023). Mykoweb.com.
Blizzard, Trent (2023). ModernForager.com.

INDEX

saddle-shaped false morel, 152
salt-loving mushroom, 90
sand mushroom, 114–15
Sarcodon imbricatus, 49
Scleroderma genus, 32, 33
shaggy mane, 68–69, 71
shaggy parasol, 86, 97–98
sheep's polypore, 43
Shiitake mushroom, 59, 144
shingled hedgehog, 49
short-stalked slippery jack bolete, 15
short-stemmed russula, 79–80
shrimp russula, xxvii, 72, 75–76, 82, 83
slippery jacks, xxvii
stinkhorn, 21
stomach irritants, 145
stubby brittlegill, 79–80
Suillus
    about, 9
    brevipes, 15
    lakei, 14
    tomentosus, 16
sulfer tuft, 160–61
sweet tooth polypore, 50
swollen-stalked cat, 117–18

tacky green russula, 81–82
tailings, xxiv–xxv
taxonomy of fungi, xxiii–xxiv
tin cap amanita, 107, 108
tooth fungi
    about, 47–48
    coral tooth, 51
    hawk's wing, 49, 52–53
    hedgehog, xxviii, 50
    recipes, 52–53

toxins in mushrooms, 144–45
    See also poisonous mushrooms
Trametes versicolor, 45
tree ears, 144
trees, xxvi–xxviii
Tremella mesenterica, 57–58
Tricholoma
    about, 110–11
    caligatum, 113
    equestre, 116
    focale, 113
    murrillianum, 112–13
    populinum, 114–15
    recipes, 128–30
truncated club, 65
turkey tail polypore, 45, 46

under-cooked mushrooms, 143

velvet foot/velvet shank, 121–22

water sources, xxii
weed killers, xxv, 143
white button, 86
white king bolete, xxvii, 13
white morel, 21
wild enoki, xxvii
wildlife, xvi–xvii
winter mushroom, 121–22
woodland agaricus, 95–96

yellow knight, 116
yellow morel, 21, 22–23
yellow ramaria, 62–63
yellow stainer, 159

ABOUT THE EDITOR

Ed Lubow has been hunting mushrooms since the 1970s, has been a member of the Colorado Mycological Society (CMS) since the 1980s, and was president of CMS twice (1997, 2010). Ed has been volunteering in the Sam Mitchel Herbarium of Fungi at Denver Botanic Gardens since 2008 and has taught the basic mushroom identification class for Denver Botanic Gardens since 2015.